Alexander Leighton

**Romances of the Old Town of Edinburgh**

Alexander Leighton

**Romances of the Old Town of Edinburgh**

ISBN/EAN: 9783744774796

Printed in Europe, USA, Canada, Australia, Japan

Cover: Foto ©ninafisch / pixelio.de

More available books at **www.hansebooks.com**

# ROMANCES OF THE OLD TOWN

OF

# EDINBURGH.

BY

ALEXANDER LEIGHTON,

AUTHOR OF "MYSTERIOUS LEGENDS OF EDINBURGH," "CURIOUS STORIED
TRADITIONS OF SCOTTISH LIFE," ETC.

EDINBURGH:
WILLIAM P. NIMMO.
1867.

# PREFACE.

THE stories in this volume owe their publication to the favour extended to my Book of Legends. If I had any apology to make it could only—independently of what is due for demerits which the cultivators of "the gay science" will not fail to notice—consist in an answer to the charge that books of this kind feed a too natural appetite for images and stimulants which tends to voracity, and which again tends to that attenuation of the mental constitution deserving of the name of *marasmus*. I may be saved the necessity of such an apology by reminding the reader that, although I plead guilty to the charge of invention, I have generally so much of a foundation for these stories as to entitle them to be withdrawn from the category of fiction. On this subject the reader may be inclined to be more particular in his inquiry than suits the possibility of an answer which may at once be safe and satisfactory. I would prefer to repose upon the generous example of that philanthropic showman, who leaves to those who look through his small windows the choice of selecting his great duke out of two personages, both worthy of the honour. The reader may believe, or not believe, but it is not imperative that he should do either; for even at the best—begging pardon of my fair readers for the Latin—*fides semper est invidens in re testificata.*

A. L.

York Lodge, Trinity,
    *January* 1867.

# CONTENTS.

|  | PAGE |
|---|---|
| THE STORY OF THE TWO RED SLIPPERS, | 1 |
| THE STORY OF THE DEAD SEAL, | 13 |
| THE STORY OF MRS HALLIDAY, | 35 |
| THE STORY OF MARY BROWN, | 60 |
| THE STORY OF THE MERRILLYGOES, | 88 |
| THE STORY OF THE SIX TOES, | 115 |
| THE STORY OF MYSIE CRAIG, | 137 |
| THE STORY OF PINCHED TOM, | 160 |
| THE STORY OF THE IRON PRESS, | 177 |
| THE STORY OF THE GIRL FORGER, | 190 |
| THE STORY OF MARY MOCHRIE AND THE MIRACLE OF THE COD, | 214 |
| THE STORY OF THE PELICAN, | 238 |
| THE STORY OF DAVIE DEMPSTER'S GHAIST, | 255 |
| THE STORY OF THE GORTHLEY TWINS, | 277 |
| THE STORY OF THE CHALK LINE, | 299 |

# ROMANCES

OF THE

# OLD TOWN OF EDINBURGH.

## The Story of the Two Red Slippers.

THE taking down of the old house of four or five flats, called Gowanlock's Land, in that part of the High Street which used to be called the Luckenbooths, has given rise to various stories connected with the building. Out of these I have selected a very strange legend—so strange, indeed, that, if not true, it must have been the production, *quod est in arte summa*, of a capital inventor; nor need I say that it is of much importance to talk of the authenticity of these things, for the most authentic are embellished by invention, and it is certainly the best embellished that live the longest; for all which we have very good reasons in human nature.

Gowanlock's Land, it would seem, merely occupied the site of an older house, which belonged, at the time of Prince Charlie's occupation of the city, to an old town councillor of the name of Yellowlees. This older house was also one of many stories, an old form in Edinburgh, supposed to have been adopted from the French; but it had, which was not uncommon, an entry from the street running under an arch, and leading to the back of the premises to the lower part of the tenement, that part occupied by the councillor. There was a lower flat, and one above, which thus constituted an entire house; and which, moreover, rejoiced in the privilege of having an extensive garden, running down as far as the sheet of water called the North Loch, that secret "domestic witness," as the ancients used to say, of many of the dark crimes of the old city. These gardens were the pride of the rich burghers of the time, decorated by Dutch-clipped hollies and trim boxwood walks; and in our special instance of Councillor Yellowlees's retreat, there was in addition a summer-house, or rustic bower, standing at the bottom; that is, towards the north, and close upon the loch. I may mention also, that in consequence of the damp, this little bower was strewed with rushes for the very special comfort of Miss Annie Yellowlees, the only and much-petted child of the good councillor.

All which you must take as introductory to the important fact that the said Miss Annie, who, as a matter of course, was "very bonnie," as well as passing rich to be, had been, somewhat previous to the prince's entry to the town, pledged to be married to no less considerable a personage than Maister John Menelaws, a son of him of the very same name who dealt in pelts in a shop of the Canongate, and a student of medicine in the Edinburgh University; but as the councillor had in his secret soul hankerings after the prince, and the said student, John, was a red-hot royalist, the marriage was suspended, all to the inexpressible grief of our "bonnie Annie," who would not have given her John for all the Charlies and Geordies to be found from Berwick to Lerwick. On the other hand— while Annie was depressed, and forced to seek relief in solitary musings in her bower by the loch— it is just as true that "it is an ill wind that blaws naebody gude;" nay, the truth of the saying was verified in Richard Templeton, a fellow-student of Menelaws, and a rival, too, in the affections of Annie; who, being a Charlicite as well as an Annicite, rejoiced that his companion was in the meantime foiled and disappointed.

Meanwhile, and, I may say, while the domestic affairs of the councillor's house were still in this unfortunate position, the prince's bubble burst in the way which history tells us of, and thereupon out came proscriptions of terrible import, and, as fate would have it, young Templeton's name was in the bloody register; the more by reason that he had been as noisy as Edinburgh students generally are in the proclamation of his partisanship. He must fly or secrete himself, or perhaps lose a head in which there was concealed a considerable amount of Scotch cunning. He at once thought of the councillor's house, with that secluded back garden and summer-house, all so convenient for secrecy, and the envied Annie there, too, whom he might by soft wooings detach from the hated Menelaws, and make his own through the medium of the pity that is akin to love. And so, to be sure, he straightway, under the shade of night, repaired to the house of the councillor, who, being a tender-hearted man, could not see a sympathiser with the glorious cause in danger of losing his head. Templeton was received, a report set abroad that he had gone to France, and all proper measures were taken within the house to prevent any domestic from letting out the secret.

In this scheme Annie, we need hardly say, was a favouring party; not that she had any love for the young man, for her heart was still true to Menelaws, (who, however, for safety's sake, was now excluded from the house,) but that, with a filial obedience to a beloved father, she felt, with a woman's heart, sympathy for one who was in distress, and a martyr to the cause which her father loved. Need we wonder at an issue which may already be looming on the vision of those who know anything of human nature? The two young folks were thrown together. They were seldom out of each other's company. Suffering is love's opportunity, and Templeton had to plead for him not only his misfortune, but a tongue rendered subtle and winning by love's action in the heart. As the days passed, Annie saw some new qualities in the martyr-prisoner which she had not seen before; nay, the pretty little domestic attentions had the usual reflex effect upon the heart which administered them, and all that the recurring image of Menelaws could do to fight against these rising predilections was so far unavailing, that that very image waxed dimmer and dimmer, while the present object was always working through the magic of sensation. Yes, Annie Yellowlees grew day by day fonder of her *protégé*, until at length she got, as the saying goes, "over head and ears." Nay, was she not, in the long nights, busy working a pair of red slippers for the object of her new affections, and were not these so very suitable to one who, like Hercules, was reduced almost to the distaff, and who, unlike that woman-tamed hero, did not need them to be applied anywhere but to the feet?

In the midst of all this secluded domesticity, there was all that comfort which is said to come from stolen waters. Then, was there not the prospect of the proscription being taken off, and the two would be made happy? Even in the meantime they made small escapades into free space. When the moon was just so far up as not to be a tell-tale, Templeton would, either with or without Annie, step out into the garden with these very red slippers on his feet. That bower by the loch, too, was favourable to the fondlings of a secret love; nor was it sometimes less to the prisoner a refuge from the eeriness which comes of *ennui*—if it is not the same thing—under the pressure of which strange feeling he would creep out at times when Annie could not be with him; nay, sometimes when the family had gone to bed.

And now we come to a very wonderful turn in our strange story. One morning Templeton did not make his appearance in the breakfast-parlour, but of course he would when he got up and got his red slippers on. Yet he was so punctual, and Annie, who knew that her father had to go to the council-chamber, would see what was the cause of the young man's delay. She went to his bed-room door. It was open, but where was Templeton?

He was not there. He could not be out in the city; he could not be even in the garden with the full light of a bright morning sun shining on it. He was not in the house; he was not in the garden, as they could see from the windows. He was nowhere to be found, and what added to the wonder, he had taken with him his red slippers, wherever he had gone. The inmates were in wonderment and consternation, and, conduplicated evil! they could make no inquiry for one who lay under the ban of a bloody proscription.

But wonders, as we all know, generally ensconce themselves in some snug theory, and die by a kind of pleasant euthanasia; and so it was with this wonder of ours. The councillor came, as the days passed, to the conclusion that Templeton, wearied out by his long confinement, had become desperate, and had gone abroad. As good a theory as could be got, seeing that he had not trusted himself in going near his friends; and Annie, whose grief was sharp and poignant, came also to settle down with a belief which still promised her her lover, though perhaps at a long date. But, somehow or another, Annie could not explain, why, even with all the fondness he had to the work of her hands, he should have elected to expose himself to damp feet by making the love-token slippers do the duty of the pair of good shoes he had left in the bed-room.

Even this latter wonder wore away, and months and months passed on the revolving wheel which casts months, not less than moments, into that gulf we call eternity. The rigour of the Government prosecutions was relaxed, and timid sympathisers began to show their heads out of doors, but Richard Templeton never returned to claim either immunity or the woman of his affections. Nor within all this time did John Menelaws enter the house of the councillor; so that Annie's days were renounced to sadness and her nights to reveries. But at last comes the eventful "one day" of the greatest of all storytellers, Time, whereon happen his startling discoveries. Verily one day Annie had wandered disconsolately into the garden, and seated herself on the wooden form in the summer-house, where in the moonlight she had often nestled in the arms of her proscribed lover, who was now gone, it might be, for ever. Objective thought cast her into a reverie, and the reverie brought up again the images of these objects, till her heart beat with an affection renewed through a dream. At length she started up, and wishing to hurry from a place which seemed filled with images at once lovable and terrible, she felt her foot caught by an impediment whereby she stumbled. On looking down she observed some object of a reddish-brown colour, and becoming alarmed lest it might be one of the toads with which the place was sometimes invaded, she started back. Yet curiosity forced her to a closer inspection. She applied her hand to the object, and brought away one of those very slippers which she had made for Templeton. All very strange; but what may be conceived to have been her feelings when she saw, sticking up from beneath the rushes, the white skeleton of a foot which had filled that very slipper! A terrible suspicion shot through her mind. She flew to her father, and, hurrying him to the spot, pointed out to him the grim object, and showed him the slipper which had covered it. Mr Yellowlees was a shrewd man, and soon saw that, the foot being there, the rest of the body was not far away. He saw, too, that his safety might be compromised either as having been concerned in a murder or the harbourage of a rebel; and so, making caution the better part of his policy, he repaired to a sympathiser, and, having told him the story, claimed his assistance. Nor was this refused. That same night, by the light of a lamp, they exhumed the body of Templeton, much reduced, but enveloped with his clothes; only they observed that the other red slipper was wanting. On examining the body, they could trace the evidence of a sword-stab through the heart. All this they kept to themselves, and that same night they contrived to get the sexton of the Canongate to inter the body as that of a rebel who had been killed and left where it was found.

This wonder also passed away, and, as time sped, old things began to get again into their natural order. Menelaws began to come again about the house, and, as an old love, when the impediments are removed, is soon rekindled again, he and Annie became even all that which they had once been to each other. The old vows were repeated without the slightest reference being made by either party to the cause which had interfered to prevent them from having been fulfilled. It was not for Annie to proffer a reason, and it did not seem to be the wish of Menelaws to ask one. In a short time afterwards they were married.

The new-married couple, apparently happy in the enjoyment of an affection which had continued so long, and had survived the crossing of a new love, at least on one side, removed to a separate house farther up in the Lawnmarket. Menelaws had previously graduated as a doctor, and he commenced to practise as such, not without an amount of success. Meanwhile, the councillor died, leaving Annie a considerable fortune. In the course of somewhere about ten years they had five children. They at length resolved on occupying the old house with the garden, for Annie's reluctance became weakened by time. It was on the occasion of the flitting that Annie had to rummage an old trunk which Menclaws, long after the marriage, had brought from the house of his father, the dealer in pelts. There, at the bottom, covered over by a piece of brown paper, she found—what? The very slipper which matched the one she still secretly retained in her possession. *Verbum sapienti.* You may now see where the strange land lies; nor was Annie blind. She concluded in an instant, and with a horror that thrilled through her whole body, that Menclaws had murdered his rival. She had lain for ten years in the arms of a murderer. She had borne to him five children. Nay, she loved him with all the force of an ardent temperament. The thought was terrible, and she recoiled from the very possibility of living with him a moment longer. She took the fatal memorial and secreted it along with its neighbour, and having a friend at a little distance from Edinburgh, she hurried thither, taking with her her children. Her father had left in her own power a sufficiency for her support, and she afterwards returned to town. All the requests of her husband for an explanation she resisted, and indeed they were not long persisted in, for Menclaws no doubt gauged the reason of her obduracy—a conclusion the more likely that he subsequently left Scotland. I have reason to believe that some of the existing Menelaws are descended from this strange union.

## The Story of the Dead Seal.

AMONG Lord Kames's session papers there are two informations or written pleadings upon the competency of an action of damages. The law point was strange enough, but the facts set forth in explanation were much more so, amounting indeed to a story so unprecedented, that I cannot help being surprised how they have escaped the curiosity of those who love "to chronicle the strong beer" of human life and action. Mr John Dalrymple, merchant, had passed his honeymoon with his wife (whose maiden name was Jean Bisset) in his house in Warrender's Close, and was about to proceed next morning to Glasgow, to execute some commission business. They had a cheerful supper; they were both young, both healthy, and both hopeful, and surely if under these conditions they could not extract some sweets out of the orange of life, they might have little chance afterwards, when the pulp would diminish to the bitter skin which is inevitable. But the truth is, they had both very good powers of suction, and will enough to use them; and if it were not that death and life play upon the same string, one might have said that the new-married couple stood no apparent risk of any fatal interruption to their happiness.

It was accordingly in very good spirits that Mr Dalrymple set forth in the morning on his journey. We might perhaps say, that the inspiration of her love lent force to his mercantile enterprise, for somehow it would seem that all the actions of man beyond the purely selfish play round the great passion, just as the gaudy petals of the flowers are a kind of acted marriage-song round what is going on in the core of the plants; and so having arrived in Glasgow, he would be thinking about his Jean, to whom, when he got home again, he would recount the wonderful triumphs he had achieved over his competing worshippers in the Temple of Mammon. He was to be eight days away, and no doubt, according to a moderate calculation, they would appear as so many months, were it not that his business engagements would keep these days to their normal length. He was to write her every day, but as he did not know at what inn he might put up, she was not to write to him until she knew where to address him. On the day after his arrival he accordingly sent her a very loving letter, containing, we presume, as many of those kisses *à la distance* as is usual in such cases, and which in our day would make some noise in the post-office receiving-box, if they were endowed with sound. Having performed this loving duty, he continued his exertions re-inspired with the hope of receiving an answer on the morning of the day following. Then—as happy people, like the other animals, are playful—he amused himself at intervals, by conjecturing as to what kind of a letter he would get, how endearingly expressed it would be, how many "dears" there would be in it, what warmth of feeling the words would convey, and how many sighs had already been wasted for his return. We might smile at such frivolities if we were not called to remember that the most of our pleasures, if looked at through the spectacle-glass of Reason, would appear to be ridiculous.

The morning came; and, according to the statement of the waiter, the letter would arrive about breakfast time. He would thus have two or three pleasures rolled up in the same hour; he would sip coffee and nectar at the same time; his ham and egg would be sweetened by ambrosia; the pleasures of sense would be heightened by those of the fancy. All which were promises made by himself, and to himself, while he was dressing, and we cannot be sure that he did not make himself more sprightly, that he had to appear before the letter of his dear Jean. Did not Rousseau blush in presence of the great lady's dog? Do what we may, we cannot get quit of the moral influence exercised over us by even inanimate things having the power of suggesting associations. But the breakfast was set, all the eatables and drinkables were on the table, and the last thing served by the waiter was the communication that the postman had passed and had left no letter.

The circumstance was rendered more than awkward by his prior hopes and anticipations, and it had the effect, moreover, which it surely ought not to have had upon a sensible man, of taking away his appetite. That it was strange there could be no doubt, for where is the loving wife who at the end of the honeymoon would allow a post to pass without replying to a loving husband's letter?—but then he contrived to make it more strange by his efforts to satisfy himself that it was not strange at all. His reasons did not satisfy him; the humming of a Scotch air carried no conviction and produced no appetite; and the result was increased anxiety, evidenced by the hanging head and heavy eye. Again the main argument was that his or her letter had miscarried,—how *could* there be any other mode of accounting for it?—and then he hummed the air again—the breakfast standing all the time. All to be again counter-argued by the fact that during all the period he had corresponded with Glasgow, there had been no miscarriage of a letter, either to or from him. This was the doctrine of chances in the form of a stern logic, and the effect was apparent in another relapse into fear and anxiety. But Mr Dalrymple, though made a moral coward by the intensity of his affection, was withal a sensible man—a fact which he gave a good proof of, by placing more faith in brandy than logic, for having called for a little of that cordial, he put a glassful into his coffee, and thereupon felt, almost as soon as the liquor had got into his stomach, that there was really a great deal less to fear than he had thought, if the whole affair was not a mere bugbear; and what was not less remarkable, if not fortunate, the brandy, by dismissing his fears, brought back his appetite, and although he required a little longer time, he contrived to make nearly as good a breakfast as if he had been favoured with the ambrosial accompaniment which he had so hopefully promised himself.

Nor was this a small matter, for the meal served as ballast to enable him to encounter something very different from the slight adverse wind he had experienced for the last hour. He was still sitting at the table, rather pleased that he had triumphed over morbid fears, and laying out his scheme for the day, when the words, coming from behind, "A letter, sir," struck his ear as if by a slap. His hand nervously seized the proffered gift, his eyes "flew" as it were to meet the superscription. He did not know the handwriting. It was directed to the care of Messrs Robert Fleming & Co., one of the houses with which he had been doing business. So far he was relieved, even when disappointed by the absence of his wife's hand on the address. He turned it with the view to break it open, and then stopped and trembled as his eye fixed itself on a large black seal, exhibiting the death's head and crossbones of a funeral letter. Even this he soon got over, under the supposition that it was an invitation to some acquaintance's funeral sent through to him, likely, by the recommendation of his wife before she had received his true address. At length he broke it open, and read the following words :—

"DEAR SIR,—I am sorry to be under the necessity of informing you that your wife died this afternoon, between three and four, from the bursting of a blood-vessel in the lungs. You will see the propriety of starting for home as soon as you receive this melancholy intelligence.—Yours,

"A. MORGAN, F.R.C.S."

No sooner had he read this terrible communication than he was rendered as rigid as a statue. The only movement that could have been observed in him was in the fingers of the right hand, as it crumpled up the paper by the spasm of the muscles acting involuntarily. His eye was fixed without an object to claim it, and his teeth were clenched as if he had been seized by lockjaw. Conditions which we use strong words to describe, as we toil in vain after an expression which must always be inadequate, even though the words are furnished by the unhappy victim himself. We try a climax by using such expressions as "palsied brain" and so forth, all the while forgetting that we are essaying to convey a condition of inward feeling by external signs, the thing and the sign being in different categories. As he still sat under the stunning effect of the letter, the waiter entered to clear the table, but when he saw the letter in the clenched hand he retreated from the scene of a private grief, which a foreign interference would only have tended to irritate; but probably the noise of the closing door helped the reaction which comes sooner or later to all victims of moral assaults, and by and by he began to think—to see the whole details of the tragedy—to be conscious of the full extent of his misery. It was not yet time for the beginning of relief, for these conditions are subject to the law of recurrence. Like the attacks of an ague they exhaust themselves by repetition, and Nature's way is at best but a cruel process of wearing out the sensibility of the palpitating nerve.

How long these oscillations lasted before the unhappy victim was able to leave his seat, we cannot tell. But as all thought is motion, so is all motion action. He could not retreat from the inevitable destiny. He must move on in the maze of the puppets. He must face the dead body of his wife. He must bury her, if he should never be able to lay the haunting spirit of memory. All business must be suspended, to leave the soul to the energies necessary for encountering the ordeal. A certain hardness, which belongs to the last feelings of despair, enabled him, even with something like deliberation, to go through the preparations of departure; but in this he exhibited merely the regularity of a machine, which obeys the imposed power behind. At eleven o'clock he was seated in the coach, as one placed there to be moved on and on, mile by mile, to see the dead body of a wife, whose smiling face, as he had seen it last, was still busy with his fancy, and whose voice, as he had heard her sing at the parting supper, still rang in his ears.

Nor were his feelings ameliorated by the journey, to remove the tediousness of which, at that slow time, the passengers were obliged to talk even against sheer Scotch taciturnity. He sat and heard, whether he would or not, the account of one who was going to bring home a wife; of another who had been away for ten years, and who was to be met at the coach-door by one who was dying to clasp him in her arms. All which were to him as sounds in another world wide apart from that one occupied by him, where he was, as he could not but think, the one solitary inhabitant, with one dead companion by his side. By and by, as the conversation flagged, he fell into that species of monomania where the brooding spirit, doomed to bear a shock, conjures up and holds before its view the principal feature of a tragedy. That feature was the image of his Jean's face. It was paler than the palest of corpses, to suit the condition of the disease of which she had died. The lips were tinged with the blood of the fatal hemorrhage. The eyes were blank and staring, as if filled with the surprise and terror of the sudden attack. Over all, the fixedness of the muscles,— the contrast of death to the versatile movements, which were obedient to the laugh of pleasure when he last drew indescribable joy from the changes of her humour. No effort could relieve him from that one haunting image. The conversation of the party seemed to render it more steadfast—

more bright—more harrowing. Nor when he tried to realise his feelings, in the personal encounter of facing the reality, could he find in himself any promise of a power to enable him to bear up against the terrible sight. It seemed to him, as the coach moved slowly on, as if he were being dragged towards a scaffold draped in black, where he was to suffer death.

When the coach at length stopped in the High Street, he was roused as from a dream, but the consciousness was even worse than the monomaniac condition in which he had been for hours. It was twelve at night; the bell of St Giles's sounded solemnly in the stillness of the sleeping city. Every one of the passengers hurried off each to his home or inn, all glad of the release. To him it was no release; he would have ridden on and on, for days and weeks, if for nothing else than to prolong the interval, at the end of which the ordeal he feared so much awaited him. Whither now? He stood in the middle of the dark and silent street with his pormanteau in his hand, for he was really uncertain whether to proceed to his sister's house in Galloway's Close, and get her to go with him to his own house, as a kind of medium, to break the effect of the vision—or to proceed homewards alone. He turned his steps towards Galloway's Close, and soon found

## THE DEAD SEAL.

that the family had gone to bed; at least, all was dark yet. Might not his sister be at his house "sitting up" with the corpse? It was not unlikely, and so he turned and proceeded towards home, his steps being forced, as if his will had no part in his ambulation. Arriving at Warrender's Close, he stood at the foot of his own stair, and, looking up to the windows, he found here, too, all dark; nor were there any neighbours astir who might address to him some human speech, if not sympathy. The silence was as complete as the darkness, and both seemed to derive the dull charm of their power from the chamber of death. At length he forced himself, step by step, up the stairs, every moment pausing, as well from the exhaustion produced by his moral cowardice, as to listen for a stray sound of the human voice. He had now got to the landing, and, entering the dark passage leading to the door of his own flat, he groped his way along by applying his unoccupied hand to the wall. He now felt his nerves fast giving way, his heart beat audibly, his limbs shook, and though he tried to correct this fear, he felt he had no power, though naturally a man of great physical courage.

He must persevere, and a step or two more brought him to the door, which he found partially open, — a circumstance he thought strange, but could account for by supposing that there were neighbours inside—gossips who meet round death-beds to utter wise saws with dry eyes. Yet, though he listened, he heard no sounds. He now pushed open the door, and so quietly, as if he feared that a grating hinge would break the silence. The lobby was still darker than outside, and his first step was towards the kitchen, the door of which he pushed back. There was no one there,—a cruse which hung upon the wall was giving forth the smallest glimmer of a dying light. There was a red peat in the grate, smouldering into white ashes. Turning to the servant's bed, he found it unoccupied, with the clothes neatly folded down, no doubt by Peggy's careful hands, and no doubt, too, Peggy had solemn work to do " ben the house." He next crossed the lobby, partly by groping, and reached a parlour, the door of which he opened gently. Dark too, and no one within. The same process was gone through with the dining-room, and with the same negative result. The last door was that of the bed-room, where he was to encounter what he feared. It was partially open. He placed his ear to the chink and listened, but he heard nothing. There was no living voice there, and death speaks none. He pushed the door open, and looked fearfully in. A small rushlight on the side-table opposite the bed threw some flickering beams around the room, bringing out indistinctly the white curtains of the bed. He approached a little, and could discover vaguely the form of his wife lying there. Would he take up the rushlight, and, with the necessary courage, go forward and examine the features? He had arrived at the spot, and at the moment, portrayed prospectively in his waking dream during his journey, and a few steps, with the rushlight in his hand, would realise the image he had brooded over so long. He struggled with himself, but without avail. Any little courage he had been for the last few minutes trying to summon up utterly gave way. There rushed into his mind vague fancies and fears,—creatures of the darkness and the death-like stillness around him, which he could neither analyse nor stay. He even thought he heard some sound from the bed where the corpse lay,—the consequence of all which was total loss of self-possession, approaching to something like a panic, and the effect of this, again, was a retreat. He sought the door, groped his way again through the inside lobby, got to the outer door, along the outer passage, down the stair to the street.

Nor when he got there did he pull up and begin to think of the extreme pusillanimity, if not folly, of his conduct. Even if he had tried, he could only have wound up his self-crimination by the ordinary excuse—that he could not help it. The house, with its stretched corpse, deserted rooms, its darkness and silence, was frightful to him. He could not return until he found some one to accompany him; and he satisfied himself of the reasonableness of this condition by the fact that the servant herself had fled in fear from the dismal scene. He began to move, though almost involuntarily, down the Canongate, his step quick and hurried, after the manner of those who are pursued by some danger, the precise nature of which they do not stop to examine. He even found a slight relief in the muscular exertion, and thus hurrying on, he reached the Duke's Walk, and came to the heap of stones called Muschet's Cairn, from Nichol Muschet of Boghall, who there murdered his wife. With no object but movement to dispel his misery, it was indifferent to him whither he should go; and hurrying to Arthur's Seat, he began to climb the hill, regardless of the dangerous characters often encountered there at night, any one of whom he had courage enough to have throttled at the moment he was flying from what was little more than a mere phantom.

Meanwhile the moon had risen, and was illuminating at intervals the north-east side of the hill, leaving all in comparative darkness again as she got behind the thick clouds which hung heavily in the sky; but the light was of no value to one who was moved only by the impulse of a distraction. Yet, as he stood for a moment, and looked back upon the city, with that Warrender's Close in the heart of it, and that house in the close, and that room with the rushlight within the house, and that bed in the room, and that figure so still and silent in the bed, he became conscious of a circumstance which had escaped him. He found that in his wild wandering, apparently without any other aim than to allay unbearable feelings by exertion, he had been unconsciously following, step by step, the very track which he and his now lost Jean had taken in a walk of the afternoon of the Sunday preceding his departure for Glasgow. The thought thus coming as a discovery was in itself a mystery, and he felt it to be a kind of duty—though with what sanction of a higher power he knew not—to continue that same track of the Sunday walk which had been consecrated by the sweet intercourse of two loving hearts. In execution of which purpose he kept moving towards the east shoulder of the hill, and such hold had this religious fancy taken of him, that he looked about for places in the track where some part of their conversation had occurred, which, from some peculiarity in it, had remained upon his memory. Nay, so weak did he become in his devotion, that he threw himself down on the cold grass at spots where Jean had required a rest, and had leant her head upon his shoulder, and had been repaid by some note of endearment. But in these reclining postures, which assumed the form of a species of worship, he remained only till the terrible thought of his privation again rose uppermost in his mind, forcing him to start to his feet by a sudden spring, and to go on again, and brush through the whins that grew on the hill-side, as if he courted their obstruction as a relief.

It is said that our ideas produce time, and our feelings devour it; and this is true at least where the feelings are of apprehension and fear of some inevitable event to occur in the future. He had still the ordeal to pass through. The sun would rise, in the light of which he would be forced to look on the dead face, and in place of considering the time occupied by these wanderings to and fro long and weary, the moments, minutes, hours, passed with such rapidity that the moon had gone far on in her journey, and the gray streaks of dawn were opening up a view to the east, before he could realise the passage of the time which had been, as it were, swallowed up by his desire to postpone what, by the laws of nature and society, he was bound to endure. How many times he had gone round the hill and up to the top, and down to Duddingstone, and along by the village road, and in through the bog, to begin his rounds again, he could not have told. But at length the sun glared threateningly in his face. Time defied him, and at length he saw the smoke of the chimneys begin to rise from the city. The red peat he had seen in the grate of his own kitchen would at least yield none. The household gods had deserted his hearth. Death and silence now reigned there. He heard eight o'clock sound from St Giles's. The people were beginning to move in all directions— all in search of pleasure, the ultimate end of all man's exertions—and he could no longer find a refuge in darkness or distance; so he began to move in the direction of the town with the weariness and lassitude of exhaustion rendering his legs rigid and his feet heavy, in addition to the hopelessness of a stricken heart. When he got to the Watergate, he began to see faces of people whom he knew, and who knew him; but he felt no desire to speak, and they doubtless from delicacy passed, without showing any desire to stop him. At length he arrived at the head of Warrender's Close, and now he felt as if he were more submissive to the necessity of what seemed to be fate, moving his limbs with more will—even with something like a wish on his mind to put an end to a long agony. Down and down step by step, the drooping head responsive in its nods to the movement of his body; up the stair step after step deliberately, resolutely; along the outer passage; now opposite his own door. That door was now closed, giving indication that the servant, or some friend or neighbour, had been in the house since he left. He tapped gently. The door was opened almost upon the instant, and Mr John Dalrymple was immediately encompassed by the arms of a woman screaming in the exultation of immoderate joy.

"John, dear John, how delighted I am to see you,—for oh, we have been in such dreadful fear about you since Peggy found your portmanteau in the lobby; but, thank God, you are come at last, and just in time for a fine warm breakfast."

The ejaculation, or rather screaming of which words was very easy, because very natural, to Mrs Jean Dalrymple, in the happy circumstances in which she found herself after so much apprehension produced by the mystery connected with the portmanteau, but as for Mr John Dalrymple speaking even to the extent of a single syllable was out of the question, unless some angel other than she of the house had touched his lips with the fire of inspiration, in place of his receiving the kisses of his wife. And this was so far well, for he certainly would have made a bungle of any attempt at the moment to express his feelings, besides laying himself open to a heavier charge of folly than that which already stood at the wrong side of his account of wisdom, or even common sense. So quietly taking off his hat he led the way into the breakfast-parlour, where he saw the breakfast things all neatly laid, beside a glowing fire, before which lay his brindled cat, not the least happy of the three; whilst Peggy, who had some forgotten thing to put on the table, had a pleasant smile on her face, just modified in a slight degree with a little apprehension which probably neither the master nor mistress could comprehend.

"I will tell you, Jeannie, all about the portmanteau, and perhaps something more, when we sit down to breakfast," words which in the meantime were satisfactory to Mrs Jean; and the event they conditioned for soon arrived, for the wife was all curiosity and despatch, and Peggy all duty and attention.

The story was very soon told, nor did Mrs Jean interrupt the narrative by a single word as she sat with staring eyes and open mouth listening to the strange tale.

"There is the letter with the dead seal," said he, as he handed it over to her.

Mrs Jean read it, and then began to examine it as if she was scrutinising the form of the written words.

"That is the handwriting of Bob Balfour, my old admirer," said she, at length, with animation. "I know his hand as well as I know yours, and he has done this in revenge for your having taken me from him. I will show you proof."

And going to a cabinet she took therefrom some letters, which she handed to her husband. These proved two things: first, that the letter with the black seal, purporting to be signed by Surgeon Morgan, was in the handwriting of Balfour, though considerably disguised; and secondly, that he had been an ardent lover of Jean, and, perhaps, on that account an enemy to the man who had been fortunate enough to secure her affections and her hand.

"All clear enough; but I shall have my revenge, too!" cried the husband. "In the meantime there are some things to be explained. Why did you not write?"

"I wrote to you last night," said Jean. "You had posted your letter too late."

"And why was not Peggy in the house last night at twelve, when I came home?"

"Peggy must answer that herself," answered Mrs Jean, smiling, and looking from her husband to Peggy, and from Peggy to her husband, as she spoke; "but I think I know what her answer will be."

And that answer was indeed very simple, amounting to no more than the very natural fact that Peggy, after her mistress had retired to rest, had gone up the common stair to Widow Henderson's, whose son Jock was courting Peggy at the time with all commendable assiduity, and considerable chance of success.

But our story, though thus so satisfactorily explained, is not yet done. Nay, as we have said, its termination was in the court, where Mr Dalrymple sued Balfour for damages and *solatium* for his cowardly and cruel act. Nor was this action itself an ordinary matter, for it interested the lawyers of the day, not by the romantic facts which led to it, but the legal principles which flowed out of it. Balfour's counsel objected to the relevancy, that is, denied there was in a lie or practical joke any cause of action. This defence gave rise to the informations we have mentioned, for the point raised was new and difficult. It was argued by Balfour that lies in the form of hoaxes are told every day, some good and some bad. Men know this, and ought to be upon their guard, which can be their only security,—for if such lies were actionable, one-half of society would be at law with the other. And as for any injury inflicted on Mr Dalrymple, it was doubtful whether the pleasure he experienced that morning when enclosed in the arms of his wife, did not more than compensate for his prior sufferings. On the other hand the pursuer argued, that by the law of Scotland there is no wrong without a legal remedy, and that having suffered by the cruel deceit both in his feelings and in his purse, (for he left his business unfinished,) he was entitled to recover. We have been unable to find the judgment.

### The Story of Mrs Halliday.

THERE are little bits of romance spread here and there in the routine of ordinary life, but for which we should be like the fairy Aline, somewhat weary of always the same flowers blooming, and the same birds singing, and the same play of human motives and passions. They are something of the nature of episodes which, as in the case of epic poems, are often the most touching and beautiful in the whole work. Yet the beauty is seldom felt by the actors themselves, who are frequently unfortunate ; and so it is that they suffer that we may enjoy the pathos of their suffering, after it has gone through the hands of art. We are led to say this as a kind of prelude to one of those episodical dramas which occurred some eighty years ago, and for twenty of them formed a household story, as well from the singularity of the principal circumstances as from the devotion of the personages. But we must go back a little from the main incidents to introduce to the reader a certain Patrick Halliday, a general agent for the sale of English broadcloth, whose place of business was in the Lawnmarket, and dwelling-house in a tenement long called Peddie's Land, situated near the Old Assembly Close. It belongs not much to our story to say that Mr Halliday was pretty well-to-do in the world, though probably even with youth and fair looks, if he had been a poor man, he would not have secured as he did the hand of a certain young lady, at that time more remarkable than he. Her name was Julia Vallance. We know no more of her except one particular, which many people would rather be known by than by wealth, or even family honours, and that was personal beauty—not of that kind which catches the eye of the common people, and which is of ordinary occurrence, but of that superior order which, addressing itself to a cultivated taste, secures an admiration which can be justified by principles. And so it came to pass that Julia had before her marriage attained to the reputation—probably not a matter of great ambition to herself, certainly not at all times very enviable —of being the belle of the old city. Nor is this saying little, when we claim it in the face of the world as a truth that Edinburgh, in spite of its smoke, has at all times been remarkable for many varieties, dark and fair, of fine women. A result this which, perhaps, we owe to a more equal mixture of the two fine races, the Celt and Saxon, than ever took place in England. But Julia had brought her price, and her market having been made, she could afford to renounce the admiration of a gaping public in consideration of the love of a husband who was as kind to her as he was true. As regards their happiness as man and wife, we will take that in the meantime as admitted, the more by reason that in due time after the marriage they had a child; and, no doubt, they would have had many in succession had it not been for the strange occurrence which forms the fulcrum of our tale.

Apart from the family in Peddie's Land, and in no manner connected with it, either by blood or favour, was that of Mr Archibald Blair, a young man living in Writers' Court, of whom we can say little more than that he was connected with the Borgue family in the Stewartry, an advocate, and also married. We are not informed of either the name or lineage of his young wife, and far less can we say aught of the perfections or imperfections she derived from nature. We are only left to presume that if there had been no love, there would probably have been no marriage, and in this case, also, we have the fact of a child having been born to help the presumption of that which, naturally enough, may be taken as granted.

The two families, far asunder in point of grade, and equally far from any chance of acquaintanceship, went on in their several walks; nor are we entitled to say, from anything previously known of them, that they even knew of each other's existence—unless, to be sure, the reputation of Julia for her personal perfections might have come to Blair's ears as it did to many who had perhaps never seen her; but, then, the marriage of a beauty is generally the end of her fame, as it is of her maiden career; and those who, before that event, are entitled to look and admire, and, perhaps, wish to whisper their aspirations, not less than to gaze on her beauty, leave the fair one to the happy man to whom the gods have assigned her.

We must now allow four years to have passed, during all which time Patrick Halliday and his wife—still, we presume, retaining her beauty, at least in the matronly form—were happy as the day is long, or, rather we should say, as the day is short, for night is more propitious to love than day. Nothing was known to have occurred to break the harmony which had begun in love, and surely when we have, as there appeared to be here, the three requisites of happiness mentioned by the ancients—health, beauty, and wealth, there was no room for any suspicion that the good deities repented of their gifts. But all this only tended to deepen the shadows of a mystery which we are about to revive at this late period.

One day, when Patrick Halliday returned from a journey to Carlisle, he was thunderstruck by the intelligence communicated to him by his servant, that his wife had disappeared two days before, and no one could tell whither she had gone. The servant, by her own report, had been sent to Leith on a message, and had taken the daughter, little Julia, with her; and when she came back, she found the door unlocked, and her mistress gone. She had made inquiries among the neighbours, she had gone to the acquaintances of the family, she had had recourse to every one and every place where it was likely she would get intelligence of her — all to no effect. Not a single individual could even say so much as that he or she had seen her that day, and at length, wearied out by her inquiries, she had had recourse to the supposition that she had followed her husband to Carlisle.

The effect of this strange intelligence was simply stupifying. Halliday dropt into a chair, and, compressing his temples with his trembling hands, seemed to try to retain his consciousness against the echoes of words which threatened to take it away. For a time he had no power of thought, and even when the ideas began again to resume their train, their efforts were broken and wild, tending to nothing but confusion.

He put question after question to the servant, every answer throwing him back upon new suppositions, all equally fruitless. The only notion that seemed to give him any relief was, that she had gone to a distance, to some of her friends—wild enough, yet better than blank despair; and as for infidelity, the thought never once occurred to him, where there was no ground on which to rear even a doubt.

At length, on regaining something like composure, he rose from his seat, and began to walk drearily through the house. He opened his desk and found that a considerable sum of money he had left there was untouched. He next opened the press in the wall, where she kept her clothes. He could not see anything wanting—the gown was there which latterly she had been in the habit of putting on when she went out to walk with little Julia; her two bonnets, the good and the better—the one for everyday and the one for Sunday—hung upon their pegs. Her jewels, too, which were in a drawer of her cabinet, were all there, with the exception of the marriage-ring she was in the habit of wearing every day. There was nothing wanting, save her ordinary body clothes, including the fringed yellow wrapper in which, during the forenoon, she used to perform her domestic duties, and which he had often thought became her better than even her silks. Wherever she had gone, she must have departed in her undress and bareheaded—nay, her slippers must have been on her feet, for not only were they away, but the high-heeled shoes by which she replaced them when she went to walk were in the place where they usually lay.

In the midst of all this mystery, the relations and others, who had been quickened into a high-wrought curiosity by the inquiries made by the servant, dropt in one after another in the expectation that the missing wife would have returned with her husband, but they went away more astonished than before, and leaving the almost frantic husband to an increase of his apprehension and fears.

The dark night came on, and he retired to bed, there to have the horrors of a roused fancy added to the deductions of a hapless and demented reason.

In the morning he rose after a sleepless and miserable night, tried to eat a little breakfast with the playful little Julia, the image of her mother, by his side, asking him every now and then, in the midst of her prattle, what had become of mammy, rose and went forth, scarcely knowing whither to go. Directing his steps almost mechanically towards his place of business, he ascertained that his clerk knew no more of the missing wife than the others. On emerging again from his office, he was doomed to run the ordinary gauntlet of inquiries, and not less of strange looks where the inquirers seemed afraid to put the question. Others tried to read him by a furtive glance, and went away with their construction. No one could give him a word of comfort, if, indeed, he had not sometimes reason to suspect that there were of his anxious friends some who were not ill pleased that he had lost, no doubt by elopement, a wife who outshone theirs.

At length he found his way to the bailie's office, where he got some of the town constables to institute a secret search among the closes, and thus the day passed resultless and weary, leaving him to another night of misery.

Next day brought scarcely any change, except in the wider spread throughout the city of the news, which, in the circumstances, degenerated into the ordinary scandal. Nor did the husband make any endeavour to check this, by stating to any one the part of the mystery connected with the clothes—a secret which he kept to himself, and brooded over with a morbid feeling he perhaps could not have explained to himself. And that day passed also, leaving at its close an increased curiosity on the part of the public, but with no change in the conviction that the lady had merely played her husband false.

The next day was not so barren—nay, it was pregnant with a fact calculated to increase the excitement without ameliorating the scandal. On going up the High Street, Halliday met one of the officers who had been engaged in the search, and who told him that another citizen had disappeared in a not less mysterious way. The question, " Who is it ?" was put, but not answered, except by another question.

" Was Mrs Halliday acquainted with Mr Archibald Blair, advocate, in Writers' Court ?"

" No," was the answer of the husband ; " and why do you put the question ?"

" Because Mrs Blair requested me," replied the officer. " She is in great distress about her husband, and I think you had better see her."

And so thought Patrick Halliday, as he hurried away to Writers' Court, much in the condition of one who would rush into the flames to avoid the waves ; for, dreadful as the death of his beloved wife would be to him, more dreadful still was the thought that she had eloped with another man, and that man might be Archibald Blair. On reaching the house, where he was admitted upon the instant, he found a counterpart of his own domestic tragedy—everything telling the tale of weariness, anxiety, and fear ; comers and goers with lugubrious countenances ; and Mrs Blair herself in a chair the picture of that very misery he had himself endured, and was at that very moment enduring.

"Who are you?" she cried, as he approached her. "Are you come with good news or bad?"

"My name is Halliday, madam," replied he. "I understand you wish to see me."

"As much as you may perhaps wish to see me," answered the lady. "The town has been ringing for days with the news of the sudden disappearance of your wife, who is said to be——," and she faltered at the word, "very beautiful. Is it true, and on what day did she disappear?"

"Too true, madam," groaned the unhappy man. "Tuesday was the day on which she was found amissing."

"Tuesday! Oh, unfortunate day!" rejoined she. "The very one, sir, when my Archibald left me, perhaps never to return. Can you tell me," she continued, as she sobbed hysterically, "whether your wife and my husband were ever at any time acquainted? Oh, I fear your answer, but I must hear it."

"I don't think," replied he, "that my wife ever knew of the existence of your husband. Even *I* never heard of his name, though I now understand he was a promising advocate. I can, therefore, give you small satisfaction; and, I presume, I can get as little from you when I ask you, what I presume is unnecessary, whether you ever heard that my wife was in any way acquainted with Mr Blair?"

"No," replied she; "neither he nor I ever mentioned her name, nor did it once come to my ears that Archibald was ever seen in the company of any woman answering to the description of your wife."

"Most wonderful circumstance, madam," replied Halliday, into whose mind a thought at the moment came, suggested by the mystery of the left clothes. "Pray, madam," he continued, "can you draw no conclusion from Mr Blair's desk or wardrobe whether or not he had provided himself for the necessities of a journey?"

"That is the very wonder of all the wonders about this strange case, sir," she answered. "I have made a careful search, knowing the money that was in the house, and having sent and inquired whether he had drawn any from the bank, I am satisfied that he had not a penny of money upon him. As for his wardrobe, every article is there, with the exception of what he used when he went to take a walk in the morning—a light dress, with a round felt hat in place of the square one. Even his cane stands there in the lobby. Where could he have gone in such an undress, and without money?"

A pertinent question, which was just the counterpart of that which Patrick Halliday had put to himself. The resemblance between the two cases struck him as wonderful, and no doubt if he had stated to Mrs Blair the analagous facts connected with his wife's wardrobe, the untouched money, and the missing slippers, that lady would have shared in his wonder; but he felt disinclined to add to her apprehensions by acquainting her with facts which could lead to no practical use. There was sufficient community of feeling between them without going into further minutiæ, and the conversation ended with looks of fearful foreboding.

Patrick Halliday left the house of the advocate only to saunter like one broke loose from Bedlam, going hither and thither without aim; learning, as he went, that the absence of Mr Blair had got abroad abreast of his own evil, and that the public had adopted the theory that his wife and the advocate had gone off together. The conclusion was only too natural, nor would it in all likelihood have been much modified even though all the facts inferring some other solution had come to be known. Even he himself was coming gradually to see that the disappearance of the two occurring at the same time, almost at the same hour, could not be countervailed by the other facts. But behind all this there was the apparent difficulty to be overcome that two individuals so well known in a news-loving city should have been in the habit of meeting, wherever the place might be, without any one having ever seen them—nay, the almost impossible thing that a woman without a bonnet, arrayed in a yellow wrapper, and with coloured slippers on her feet, could have passed through any of the streets without being recognised, and that the same immunity from all observation should have been enjoyed by a public man so well known—dressed, too, in a manner calculated to attract notice. There was certainly another theory, and some people entertained the possibility, if not the reasonableness of it, that the two clandestine lovers might have concealed themselves for an obvious purpose in some of those houses whose keepers have an interest in the concealment of their guilty lodgers. But this theory must have appeared a very dubious one, for it involved a degree of imprudence, if not recklessness, amounting to voluntary ruin, where a little foresight might have secured their object without further sacrifice than the care required in the preservation of their guilty secret. But, unlikely as this theory was, it was not left untested, for special visits and inquiries were made in all places known as likely to offer refuge to persons in their circumstances and condition.

All was still in vain; another day passed, and

another, till the entire week proved the inutility of both search and inquiry. The ordinary age of a wonder was attained, with the usual consequence of the beginning of that decay which is inherent in all things. Yet it is with these moral organisms as with the physical—they cast their seeds to come up again as memories. A month elapsed, and then another, and another, till these periods carried the mere diluted interest of the early days. So it is that the big animal, the world, on which man is one of the small parasites, supplies the sap as the desires require, and changes it as the appetite changes, with that variety which is the law of nature. Even as regarded Patrick Halliday and Mrs Blair, the moral granulation began gradually and silently to fill up the excavated sores in their hearts, and by and by it ought by rule to have come about that the cicatrices would follow, and then the smoothing of the covering, even to the pellucid skin. And as for the public, new wonders, from the ever-discharging womb of events, were rising up every day, so that the story of the once famed Julia Halliday and the advocate Blair was at length assuming the sombre colours of one of the acted romances of life. But it takes long to make a complete romance. There is a vitality in moral events as in some physical ones which revives in overt symptoms, and so it was in the case we are concerned with. A whole year had at length passed, and brooding silence had waxed thick over the now comparatively-old event; but the silence was to be broken by the speaking of an inanimate thing as strange in itself as the old mystery.

One day, when Patrick Halliday had returned from his office in the upper part of the city to Peddie's Land for the purpose of getting a letter which he had by mistake left on the table in the morning, he found that the servant had gone out as usual for the purpose of taking little Julia for an airing; but, getting entrance by his own key, he proceeded along the lobby to the parlour, on opening the door of which, and entering, his eye was attracted to something on the floor. The room was at the time shaded by the hangings drawn together to keep out the rays of the sun, and, not distinguishing the object very well, he thought it was some plaything of Julia's. On taking it up he found, to his amazement, that it was one of the slippers of his wife. It had a damp musty smell, which he found so unpleasant that he threw it down on the floor again, and then began to think where in the world it had come from, or how it came to be there. The servant might explain it when she came in; but why she should have gone out with that remaining to be explained he could not understand. Meanwhile his only conclusion was, that sufficient search had not been made for the slippers, and that the dog, which was out with the maid, had dragged the article from some nook or corner which had escaped observation. Under this impression he felt inclined to seek for the neighbour of that which had been so strangely found, altogether oblivious of the fact that, if the slipper had been left by the runaway, she must have departed either bare-footed or in her stocking-soles; for her shoes, so far as he could know, had been accounted for.

But he was not to be called upon to make this search; something else awaited him; for, as he sat enveloped in the darkness of this new mystery, his eye, wandering about in the shaded room, was attracted by another object. Rising, as if by a start, he proceeded to the spot, and took up, to his further amazement, a man's shoe. He at first supposed that it was one of his own; but on looking at the silver buckle, on which were engraved—not an uncommon thing at the time—two initial letters, (these were " A. B.,") he was at no loss for the name. It was that of the missing advocate. This shoe, like the slipper, was covered with white mould, and smelt of an odour different from and more disagreeable than mere must. He was now in more perplexity than ever, nor could he bring his mind to a supposition of how these things came to be there. It was the time of popular superstitions, when intelligences in the shape of ghosts and hobgoblins, and all forms of good and devilish beings, seemed to have nothing else to do than to entertain themselves with the fancies, feelings, and passions of men, and we might not be surprised to find that Patrick Halliday was brought under the feeling of an indescribable awe—nay, it is doubtful if even the veritable spirits of his wife and her paramour, if they had then and there appeared in that shaded room before him, would have produced a stronger impression upon him than did those speechless yet eloquent things. A moral vertigo was on him; he threw himself again into a chair, and felt his knees knocking against each other, as if the nerves, paralysed by the deep impression upon the brain, were no longer under the influence of the will.

After sitting for a time in this state of perplexity and awe, from which he could not extricate himself, the servant, with his daughter, returned. He called her to his presence, and asked her, pointing to the shoe and the slipper, "how those things came to be there?"

The girl was seized with as great wonder as he himself had been, and there was even a greater cause for astonishment on her part, insomuch as, according to her declaration, she had cleaned out and dusted the parlour within half an hour of going forth, and these articles were certainly not in the room then. As for the outer door, she had left it fastened in the usual way, and the windows were carefully drawn down before her departure. Where *could* they have come from, she questioned both her master and herself, with an equal chance of a satisfactory answer from either. Then she would not have been a woman if she could have resisted the claims of superstition in a case so inexplicable, so extraordinary, so unparalleled even in winter fireside stories. And so she looked at her master, and he looked at her, in blank wonder, without either of them having the power of venturing even a surmise as to how or by what earthly or unearthly means those ominous things, so terrible in the associations by which they were linked to their owners, came to be where they were.

After some longer time uselessly occupied, Patrick Halliday bethought himself of going to Writers' Court, so taking up the silver-buckled shoe, and putting it into his large coat pocket, he proceeded to Mrs Blair's. He found her in that state of reconciled despondency to which she had been reduced for more than two months; but the moment she saw Patrick Halliday enter, she sprang up as if she had been quickened by the impulse of a new-born hope rising amidst the clouds of a long-settled despair. The movement was soon stayed when her keenness scanned the face of the man; but a new feeling took possession of her when she saw him draw out of his pocket the silver-buckled shoe with which she had been as familiar as with her own.

"Where, in the Lord's name!—" she cried, without being able to say more, while she seized spasmodically the strange object, still covered as it was with the mould, and with the silver obscured by the passage of time. And, gazing at it, she heard Halliday's account of how he came to be in possession of it, along with the slipper.

"Have you the neighbour in the house?" he inquired.

"No, no," said she; "but I am certain that that is one of the shoes Archibald had on the day he disappeared. Oh, sir, I can scarcely look at these initials; and there is such a death-like odour about it that it sickens me."

"It is the same with the slipper," said he. "It would seem that both of them had been taken off the feet of corpses."

"Strange mystery altogether," added she, with a deep sigh. "Oh, I could have wished I had not seen these—it only serves to renew my care, without satisfying my natural desire to know the fate of one I loved so dearly."

"It is so with me as well, madam," rejoined Mr Patrick; "but the finding of this shoe and slipper may satisfy us of the connexion between your husband and my wife."

"Yes, yes," ejaculated she; "but oh, merciful God! what a wretched satisfaction to the bereaved wife and the deserted child. You are a man, and can bear up. A poor woman must sit in solitude and mourn, while the flesh wastes day by day under the weary spirit."

"And you can suggest nothing to help me to an explanation of this new mystery?" said he.

"Nothing; all is darker than ever," replied she. "But, sir, you have got the only trace that for a long year has been found of this most unfortunate—I fear, unhappy pair, and it will be for you to improve it in some way. Something more will follow. I will go over with you myself to your house. A woman's eyes are sharper than a man's. I would like to examine the house, and judge for myself."

And the lady, rising, went and dressed herself. In a few minutes more they were on the way to Peddie's Land; probably, as they went along, objects of speculation to those who knew the strange link by which their fortunes were joined. Nor was it unlikely that evil tongues might suggest that as their partners had played them false, they intended to make amends by a kind of poetical retribution. Alas! how different from their thoughts, how unlike their feelings, how far distant from their object!

On arriving at the house, a new wonder was to meet them, almost upon the threshold. The servant ran forward to Halliday, holding in her hand the partner of the silver-buckled shoe which her master had in his pocket. She was utterly unable to say a word, her eyes were strained not less in width than in intensity, her mouth was open like that of an idiot, and motioning and muttering, "Come, come," she led her master and Mrs Blair on through two or three rooms till she came to a small closet, at the back of which there was a door, now for the first time in Patrick Halliday's experience found open. In explanation of which peculiarity we require to suspend our narrative for a minute or two, to enable us to inform the reader, that the house then occupied by Halliday had, five years before, and immediately preceding his marriage, been in possession of George Morgan, a wool-dealer.

Morgan's warehouse, where he stored his wool, entered from a close to the west, through a pend, between Peddie's Land and the large tenement adjoining. The run of the warehouse was thus at right angles to that of the dwelling-house, and

Morgan was thereby enabled to knock out a small door at the back of a press, through which he could conveniently pass to his place of business without being at the trouble of going down the close to the main entry. After Morgan's death, the house and warehouse went to his heirs, from whom Halliday rented the former, the other having been let to some other person for three years, after which it had been without a tenant. We may state also that Halliday was at first quite aware of the existence of the door at the back of the press, and had even taken the precaution of getting it locked; but as no requisition had been made by the tenant of the warehouse to have the communication more securely barred, the door had been left in the condition we have described.

Resuming our story: the servant, when she came to the point where we left her, stopped and trembled; but by this time Halliday had begun to see whither these pointings tended, and pushing the girl aside with a view to examine the door, he was astonished to find that it opened to his touch—a fact better known by Nettle, his dog, who had, as the shoes testified, been there before.

On entering the warehouse, all the windows of which were shut except one, through which a ray of light struggled to illuminate merely a part of the room, the party beheld a sight which in all likelihood would retain a vividness in their memories after all other images of earthly things had passed away. Right in the middle of the partial light admitted by the solitary window lay the bodies of two persons—a man and a woman. The latter had on her a yellow morning gown trimmed with green. One slipper was on, the other off; her head, which was uncovered, was surmounted by the high toupee of the times, which consisted of the collected hair brushed up and supported by a concealed cushion. The man had on a morning dress, with a round felt hat, which still retained its place on his head. There was no corruption in the bodies of that kind called moist. They were nearly shrivelled, but that to an extent which reduced them to little other than skeletons covered with a brown skin—a state of the bodies which probably resulted from the dry air of the warcroom, heated as it was by a smithy being immediately below it, the smoke of which was conveyed by a flue up the side of the tenement. The two bodies lay clasped in each other's arms, the faces were so close that the noses almost met; the eyes were open, and though the balls were shrunk so much that they could not be seen, the lids, which had shrunk also, were considerably apart. These were the bodies of Julia Halliday and Archibald Blair.

There was not a word spoken by the searchers.

Their eyes told them all that was necessary to convince them of the identity of those who lay before them. Nor, when Halliday took up a paper which lay at the head of Blair, did he think it necessary to make any observation of surprise at what was in keeping with what they saw.

"Oh, read," said Mrs Blair, as she gasped in the midst of her agony.

Halliday, holding up the paper so as to receive the light, read as follows:—

"Whoever you may be, man or woman, who first discovers the bodies of me and her who lies by my side will please, as he or she hopes for mercy, deliver this paper either to Mr Patrick Halliday of Peddie's Land, or Mrs Archibald Blair in Writers' Court, that they may take the means of getting us decently interred. Julia Halliday and I, Archibald Blair, met and looked and loved. These few words contain the secret of our misfortune, and must be the excuse of our crime in taking away our lives. Our love was too strong to be quelled by resolution, too sacred to be corrupted by coarse enjoyment of the senses, too hopeless to be borne amidst the impediments of our mutual obligations to our spouses. We felt and believed that it was only our mortal bodies that belonged to our partners, our spirits were ours and ours alone by that decree which made the soul, with its sympathies and its elections, before ever the world was, or marriage, which is only a convention of man's making. We loved, we sinned not, yet we were unhappy, because we could not fulfil the obligations of affection to those we had sworn at the altar to love and honour. Often have we torn ourselves from each other with vows on our lips of mutual avoidance, but these efforts were vain. We could not live estranged, and we flew again to each other's arms, again to vow, again to meet, again to be blessed, again to be tortured. This life was unendurable; and, left to the alternative of parting or dying, we selected the latter. The poison was bought by me in two separate vials. As I write, Julia holds hers in her hands, and smiles as she is about to swallow the drug. We have resolved to lie down face to face, so as to be able to look into each other's eyes and watch jealously Death as he drags us slowly from each other. I have now swallowed my draft, smiling the while in Julia's face. She does the same. The pen trembles in my hand. Farewell, my wife: Julia mutters, 'Farewell, my husband.' Against neither have we ever sinned.

"ARCHIBALD BLAIR."

## The Story of Mary Brown.

IF the reader of what I am going to relate for his or her edification, or for perhaps a greater luxury, viz., wonder, should be so unreasonable as to ask for my authority, I shall be tempted, because a little piqued, to say that no one should be too particular about the source of pleasure, inasmuch as, if you will enjoy nothing but what you can prove to be a reality, you will, under good philosophical leadership, have no great faith in the sun—a thing which you never saw, the existence of which you are only assured of by a round figure of light on the back of your eye, and which may be likened to tradition; so all you have to do is to believe like a good Catholic, and be contented, even though I begin so poorly as to try to interest you in two very humble beings who have been dead for many years, and whose lives were like a steeple without a bell in it, the intention of which you cannot understand till your eye reaches the weathercock upon the top, and then you wonder at so great an erection for so small an object. The one bore the name of William Halket, a young man, who, eight or nine years before he became of much interest either to himself or any other body, was what in our day is called an Arab of the City —a poor street boy, who didn't know who his father was, though, as for his mother, he knew her by a pretty sharp experience, insomuch as she took from him every penny he made by holding horses, and gave him more cuffs than cakes in return. But Bill got out of this bondage by the mere chance of having been taken a fancy to by Mr Peter Ramsay, innkeeper and stabler, in St Mary's Wynd, (an ancestor, we suspect, of the Ramsays of Barnton,) who thought he saw in the City Arab that love of horse-flesh which belongs to the Bedouin, and who accordingly elevated him to the position of a stable-boy, with board and as many shillings a week as there are days in that subdivision of time.

Nor did William Halket — to whom for his merits we accord the full Christian name—do any discredit to the perspicacity of his master, if it was not that he rather exceeded the hopes of his benefactor, for he was attentive to the horses, civil to the farmers, and handy at anything that came in his way. Then, to render the connexion reciprocal, William was gratefully alive to the conviction that if he had not been, as it were, taken from the street, the street might have been taken from him, by his being locked up some day in the Heart of Midlothian. So things went on in St Mary's Wynd for five or six years, and might have gone on for twice that period, had it not been that at a certain hour of a certain day William fell in love with a certain Mary Brown, who had come on that very day to be an under-housemaid in the inn; and strange enough, it was a case of "love at first sight," the more by token that it took effect the moment that Mary entered the stable with a glass of whisky in her hand sent to him by Mrs Ramsay. No doubt it is seldom that a fine blooming young girl, with very pretty brown hair and very blue eyes, appears to a young man with such a recommendation in her hand, but we are free to say that the whisky had nothing to do with an effect which is well-known to be the pure result of the physical attributes of the individual. Nay, our statement might have been proved by the counterpart effect produced upon Mary herself, for she was struck by William at the same moment when she handed him the glass; and we are not to assume that the giving of a pleasant boon is always attended with the same effect as the receiving of it.

But, as our story requires, it is the love itself

between these two young persons whose fates were so remarkable we have to do with—not the causes, which are a mystery in all cases. Sure it is, humble in position as they were, they could love as strongly, as fervently, perhaps as ecstatically, as great people—nay, probably more so, for education has a greater chance of moderating the passion than increasing it; and so, notwithstanding of what Plutarch says of the awfully consuming love between Phrygius and Picrea, and also what Shakespeare has sung or said about a certain Romeo and a lady called Juliet, we are certain that the affection between these grand personages was not *more* genuine, tender, and true than that which bound the simple and unsophisticated hearts of Will Halket and Mary Brown. But at best we merely play on the surface of a deep subject when we try with a pen to describe feelings, and especially the feelings of love. We doubt, if even the said pen were plucked from Cupid's wing, it would help us much. We are at best only left to a choice of expressions, and perhaps the strongest we could use are those which have already been used a thousand times—the two were all the world to each other, the world outside nothing at all to them; so that they could have been as happy on the top of Mount Ararat, or on the island of Juan Fernandez, provided they should be always in each other's company, as they were in St Mary's Wynd. And as for whispered protestations and chaste kisses—for really their love had a touch of romance about it you could hardly have expected, but which yet kept it pure, if not in some degree elevated above the loves of common people — these were repeated so often about the quiet parts of Arthur's Seat and the Queen's Park, and the fields about the Dumbiedykes and Duddingstone Loch, that they were the very moral aliments on which they lived. In short, to Mary Brown the great Duke of Buccleuch was as nothing compared to Willie Halket, and to Willie Halket the beautiful Duchess of Grammont would have been as nothing compared to simple Mary Brown. All which is very amiable and very necessary, for if it had been so ordained that people should feel the exquisite sensations of love in proportion as they were beautiful, or rich, or endowed with talent, (according to a standard,) our world would have been even more queer than that kingdom described by Gulliver, where the ugliest individual is made king or queen.

Things continued in this very comfortable state at the old inn in St Mary's Wynd for about a year, and it had come to enter into the contemplation of Will that upon getting an increase of his wages he would marry Mary and send her to live with her mother, a poor hard-working washerwoman, in Big Lochend Close; whereunto Mary was so much inclined, that she looked forward to the day as the one that promised to be the happiest that she had yet seen, or would ever see. But, as an ancient saying runs, the good hour is in no man's choice; and about this time it so happened that Mr Peter Ramsay, having had a commission from an old city man, a Mr Dreghorn, located as a planter in Virginia, to send him out a number of Scottish horses, suggested to William that he would do well to act as supercargo and groom. Mr Dreghorn had offered to pay a good sum to the man who should bring them out safe, besides paying his passage over and home. And Mr Ramsay would be ready to receive Will into his old place again on his return. As for Mary, with regard to whom the master knew his man's intentions, she would remain where she was, safe from all temptation, and true to the choice of her heart. This offer pleased William, because he saw that he could make some money out of the adventure, whereby he would be the better able to marry, and make a home for the object of his affections; but he was by no means sure that Mary would consent; for women, by some natural divining of the heart, look upon delays in affairs of love as ominous and dangerous. And so it turned out that one Sabbath evening, when they were seated beneath a tree in the King's Park, and William had cautiously introduced the subject to her, she was like other women.

"The bird that gets into the bush," she said, as the tears fell upon her cheeks, "sometimes forgets to come back to the cage again. I would rather hae the lean lintie in the hand than the fat finch on the wand."

"But you forget, Mary, love," was the answer of Will, "that you can feed the lean bird, but you can't feed me. It is I who must support you. It is to enable me to do that which induces me to go. I will come with guineas in my pocket where there are now only pennies and placks, and you know, Mary, the Scotch saying, 'A heavy purse makes a light heart.'"

"And an unsteady one," rejoined Mary. "And you may bring something else wi' you besides the guineas; may be, a wife."

"One of Mr Dreghorn's black beauties," said Will, laughing. "No, no, Mary, I am too fond of the flaxen ringlets, the rosy cheeks, and the blue eyes, and you know, Mary, you have all these, so you have me in your power. But to calm your fears and stop your tears I'll tell you what I'll do."

"Stay at hame, Will, and we'll live and dee thegither."

"No," replied Will, "but, like the genteel lover I have read of, I will swear on your Bible that I will return to you within the year, and marry you at the Tron Kirk, and throw my guineas into the lap of your marriage-gown, and live with you until I die."

For all which and some more we may draw upon our fancy, but certain it is, as the strange story goes, that Will did actually then and there—for Mary had been at the Tron Kirk and had her Bible in her pocket, (an article the want of which is not well supplied by the scent-bottle of our modern Marys,)—swear to do all he had said, whereupon Mary was so far satisfied that she gave up murmuring—perhaps no more than that. Certain also it is that before the month was done, Will, with his living kicking charges, and after more of these said tears from Mary than either of them had arithmetic enough to enable them to count, embarked at Leith for Richmond, at which place the sugar-planter had undertaken to meet him.

We need say nothing of the voyage across the Atlantic—somewhat arduous at that period—nor need we pick up Will again till we find him in Richmond with his horses all safe, and as fat and sleek as if they had been fed by Neptune's wife, and had drawn her across in place of her own steeds. There he found directions waiting from Mr Dreghorn to the effect that he was to proceed with the horses to Peach Grove, his plantation, a place far into the heart of the country; but Will was content, for had he not time and to spare within the year, and he would see some more of the new world, which, so far as his experience yet went, seemed to him to be a good place for a freeman to live in. So off he went, putting up at inns by the way as well supplied with food and fodder as Mr Peter Ramsay's, in St Mary's Wynd, and showing off his nags to the planters, who wondered at their bone and muscle, the more by reason they had never seen Scotch horses before. As he progressed, the country seemed to Will more and more beautiful, and by the time he reached Peach Grove he had come to the unpatriotic conclusion that all it needed was Mary Brown, with her roses, and ringlets, and eyes, passing like an angel — lovers will be poets — among these ebon beauties, to make it the finest country in the world.

Nor when the Scotsman reached Peach Grove did the rosy side of matters recede into the shady, for he was received in a great house by Mr Dreghorn with so much kindness, that, if the horses rejoiced in maize and oats, Will found himself, as the saying goes, in five-bladed clover. But more awaited him, even thus much more, that the planter, and his fine lady of a wife as well, urged him to remain on the plantation, where he would be well paid and well fed; and when Will pleaded his engagement to return to Scotland within the year, the answer was ready that he might spend eight months in Virginia at least, which would enable him to take home more money—an answer that seemed so very reasonable, if not prudent, that "Sawny" saw the advantage thereof and agreed. But we need hardly say that this was conceded upon the condition made with himself, that he would write to Mary all the particulars, and also upon the condition acceded to by Mr Dreghorn, that he would take the charge of getting the letter sent to Scotland.

All which having been arranged, Mr Halket—for we cannot now continue to take the liberty of calling him Will—was forthwith elevated to the position of driving negroes in place of horses, an occupation which he did not much relish, insomuch that he was expected to use the lash, an instrument of which he had been very chary in his treatment of four-legged chattels, and which he could not bring himself to apply with anything but a sham force in reference to the two-legged species. But this objection he thought to get over by using the sharp crack of his Jehu-voice, as a substitute for that of the whip; and in this he persevered, in spite of the jeers of the other drivers, who told him the thing had been tried often, but that the self-conceit of the negro met the stimulant and choked it at the very entrance to the car; and this he soon found to be true. So he began to do as others did, and he was the sooner reconciled to the strange life into which he had been precipitated by the happy condition of the slaves themselves, who, when their work was over, and at all holiday hours, dressed themselves in the brightest colours of red and blue and white, danced, sang, ate corn-cakes and bacon, and drank coffee with a zest which would have done a Scotch mechanic, with his liberty to produce a lock-out, much good to see. True, indeed, the white element of the population was at a discount at Peach Grove. But in addition to the above source of reconciliation, Halket became day by day more captivated by the beauty of the country, with its undulating surface, its wooded clumps, its magnolias, tulip-trees, camellias, laurels, passion-flowers, and palms, its bright-coloured birds, and all the rest of the beauties for which it is famous all over the world. But nature might charm as it might—Mary Brown was three thousand miles away.

Meanwhile the time passed pleasantly, for he was accumulating money, Mary's letter would be on the way, and the hope of seeing her within the appointed time was dominant over all the fascinations which charmed the senses. But when the month came in which he ought to have received a letter, no letter came—not much this to be thought of, though Mr Dreghorn tried to impress him with the idea that there must be some change of sentiment in the person from whom he expected the much-desired answer. So Halket wrote again, giving the letter, as before, to his master, who assured him it was sent carefully away, and while it was crossing the Atlantic he was busy in improving his penmanship and arithmetic, under the hope held out to him by his master that he would, if he remained, be raised to a book-keeper's desk; for the planter had seen early that he had got hold of a long-headed, honest, sagacious "Sawny," who would be of use to him. On with still lighter wing the intermediate time sped again, but with no better result in the shape of an answer from her who was still the object of his day fancies and his midnight dreams. Nor did all this kill his hope. A third letter was despatched, but the returning period was equally a blank. We have been counting by months, which, as they sped, soon brought round the termination of his year, and with growing changes too in himself, for as the notion began to worm itself into his mind that his beloved Mary was either dead or faithless, another power was quietly assailing him from within, no other than ambition in the most captivating of all shapes, Mammon. We all know the manner in which the golden deity acquires his authority, nor do we need to have recourse to the conceit of the old writer who tells us that the reason why gold has such an influence upon man lies in the fact that it is of the colour of the sun, which is the fountain of light, and life, and joy. Certain it is, at least, that Halket having been taken into the counting-house on a raised salary, began " to lay by," as the Scotch call it, and by and by, with the help of a little money lent to him by his master, he began by purchasing produce from the neighbouring plantations, and selling it where he might, all which he did with advantage, yet with the ordinary result to a Scotsman, that while he turned to so good account the king's head, the king's head began to turn his own.

And now in place of months we must begin to count by lustrums, and the first five years, even with all the thoughts of his dead, or, at least, lost Mary, proved in Halket's case the truth of the book written by a Frenchman, to prove that a man is a plant, for he had already thrown out from his head or heart so many roots in the Virginian soil that he was bidding fair to be as firmly fixed in his new sphere as a magnolia, and if that bore golden blossoms, so did he; yet, true to his first love, there was not among all these flowers one so fair as the fair-haired Mary. Nay, with all hope not yet extinguished, he had even at the end of the period resolved upon a visit to Scotland, when strangely enough, and sadly too, he was told by Mr Dreghorn that having had occasion to hear from Mr Peter Ramsay on the subject of some more horse dealings, that person had reported to him that Mary Brown, the lover of his old stable-boy, was dead. A communication this which, if it had been made at an earlier period, would have prostrated Halket altogether, but it was softened by his long foreign anticipations, and he was thereby the more easily inclined to resign his saddened soul to the further dominion of the said god, Mammon, for as to the notion of putting any of those beautiful half-castes he sometimes saw about the planter's house at Peach Grove, in the place of her of the golden ringlets, it was nothing better than the desecration of a holy temple. Then the power of the god increased with the offerings, one of which was his large salary as manager, a station to which he was elevated shortly after he had received the doleful tidings of Mary's death. Another lustrum is added, and we arrive at ten years, and yet another, and we come to fifteen; at the end of which time Mr Dreghorn died, leaving Halket as one of his trustees, for behoof of his wife, in whom the great plantation vested. If we add yet another lustrum, we find the Scot—fortunate, save for one misfortune that made him a joyless worshipper of gold—purchasing from the widow, who wished to return to England, the entire plantation under the condition of an annuity.

And Halket was now rich, even beyond what he had ever wished, but the chariot-wheels of Time would not go any slower—nay, they moved faster, and every year more silently, as if the old Father had intended to cheat the votary of Mammon into a belief that he would live for ever. The lustrums still passed: another five, another, and another, till there was scope for all the world being changed, and a new generation taking the place of that with which William Halket and Mary Brown began; and he was changed too, for he began to take on those signs of age which make the old man a painted character; but in one thing he was not changed, and that was the worshipful steadfastness, the sacred fidelity, with which he still treasured in his mind the form and face, the words and the smiles, the nice and refined peculiarities that feed love as with nectared sweets, which once belonged to Mary Brown, the first creature that had moved his affections, and the last to hold them, as the object of a cherished memory for ever. Nor with time so deceptive, need we be so sparing in dealing out those periods of five years, but say at once that at last William Halket could count twelve of them since first he set his foot on Virginian soil: yea, he had been there for sixty summers, and he had now been a denizen of the world for seventy-eight years. In all which our narrative has been strange, but we have still the stranger fact to set forth, that at this late period he was seized with that moral disease (becoming physical in time) which the French call *mal du pays*, the love of the country where one was born and first enjoyed the fresh springs that gush from the young heart. Nor was it the mere love of country, as such, for he was seized with a particular wish to be where Mary lay in the churchyard of the Canongate, to erect a tombstone over her, to seek out her relations and enrich them, to make a worship out of a disappointed love, to dedicate the last of his thoughts to the small souvenirs of her humble life. Within a month this old man was on his way to Scotland, having sold the plantation, and taken bills with him to an amount of little less than a hundred thousand pounds.

In the course of five weeks William Halket put his foot on the old pier of Leith, on which some very old men were standing, who had been urchins when he went away. The look of the old harbour revived the image which had been imprinted on his mind when he sailed, and the running of the one image into the other produced the ordinary illusion of all that long interval appearing as a day; but there was no illusion in the change, that Mary Brown was there when he departed, and there was no Mary Brown there now. Having called a coach he told the driver to proceed up Leith Walk, and take him to Peter Ramsay's Inn, in St Mary's Wynd; but the man told him there was no inn there, nor had been in his memory. The man added that he would take him to the White Horse in the Canongate, and thither accordingly he drove him. On arriving at the inn he required the assistance of the waiter to enable him to get out of the coach, nor probably did the latter think this any marvel, after looking into a face so furrowed with years, so pale with the weakness of a languid circulation, so saddened with care. The rich man had only an inn for a home, nor in all his native country was there one friend whom he hoped to find alive. Neither would a search help him, as he found on the succeeding day, when, by the help of his staff, he essayed an infirm walk in the great thoroughfare of the old city. The houses were not much altered, but the signboards had got new names and figures, and as for the faces, they were to him even as those in

Crete to the Cretan, after he awoke from a sleep of forty-seven years—a similitude only true in this change, for Epimenidas was still as young when he awoke as when he went to sleep, but William Halket was old among the young and the grown, who were unknown to him as he was indeed strange to them. True, too, as the coachman said, Peter Ramsay's Inn, where he had heard Mary singing at her work, and the stable where he had whistled blithely among his favourite horses, were no longer to be seen—*etiam cineres perierunt*—their very sites were occupied by modern dwellings. What of that small half-sunk lodging in Big Lochend Close, where Mary's mother lived, and where Mary had been brought up, where perhaps Mary had died. Would it not be a kind of pilgrimage to hobble down the Canongate to that little lodging, and might there not be for him a sad pleasure even to enter and sit down by the same fireplace where he had seen the dearly-beloved face, and listened to her voice, to him more musical than the melody of angels?

And so after he had walked about till he was wearied, and his steps became more unsteady and slow, and as yet without having seen a face which he knew, he proceeded in the direction of the Big Close. There was, as regards stone and lime, little change here; he soon recognised the half-sunk window where, on the Sunday evenings, he had sometimes tapped as a humorous sign that he was about to enter, which had often been responded to by Mary's finger on the glass, as a token that he would be welcome. It was sixty years since then. A small corb would now hold all that remained of both mother and daughter. He turned away his head as if sick, and was about to retrace his steps. Yet the wish to enter that house rose again like a yearning, and what more in the world than some souvenir of the only being on earth he ever loved was there for him to yearn for? All his hundred thousand pounds were now, dear as money had been to him, nothing in comparison of the gratification of seeing the room where she was born—yea, where probably she had died. In as short a time as his trembling limbs would carry him down the stair, which, in the ardour of his young blood he had often taken at a bound, he was at the foot of it; there was there the old familiar dark passage, with doors on either side, but it was the farthest door that was of any interest to him. Arrived at it he stood in doubt. He would knock, and he would not; the mystery of an undefined fear was over him, and yet, what had he to fear, for half a century the inmates had been changed, no doubt, over and over again, and he would be as unknowing as unknown? At length the trembling finger achieves the furtive tap, and the door was opened by a woman, whose figure could only be seen by him in coming between him and the obscure light that came in by the half-sunk window in front; nor could she, even if she had had the power of vision, see more of him, for the lobby was still darker.

"Who may live here?" said he, in the expectation of hearing some name unknown to him.

The answer, in a broken cracked voice, was not slow—

"Mary Brown; and what may you want of her?"

"Mary Brown!" but not a word more could he say, and he stood as still as a post, not a movement of any kind did he show for so long a time that the woman might have been justified in her fear of a very spirit.

"And can ye say nae mair, sir?" rejoined she. "Is my name a bogle to terrify human beings?"

But still he was silent, for the reason that he could not think—far less speak, nor even for some minutes could he achieve more than the repetition of the words, "Mary Brown."

"But hadna ye better come in, good sir?" said she. "Ye may ken our auld saying: 'They that speak in the dark may miss their mark;' for words carry nae light in their een ony mair than me, for, to say the truth, I am old and blind."

And, moving more as an automaton than as one under a will, Halket was seated on a chair with this said old and blind woman by his side, who sat silent and with blank eyes waiting for the stranger to explain what he wanted. Nor was the opportunity lost by Halket, who, unable to understand how she should have called herself Mary Brown, began, in the obscure light of the room, to scrutinise her form and features, and in doing this he went upon the presumption that this second Mary Brown only carried the name of the first; but as he looked he began to detect features which riveted his eyes; where the re-agent was so sharp and penetrating, the analysis was rapid—it was also hopeful—it was also fearful. Yes, it was true that that woman was *his* Mary Brown. The light-brown ringlets were reduced to a white stratum of thin hair; the blue eyes were gray, without light and without speculation; the roses on the cheeks were replaced by a pallor, the forerunner of the colour of death; the lithe and sprightly form was a thin spectral body, where the sinews appeared as strong cords, and the skin seemed only to cover a skeleton. Yet withal he saw in her that identical Mary Brown. That wreck was dear to him; it was a relic of the idol he had worshipped through life; it was the only remnant in the world which had any interest for him; and he could on the instant have clasped her to his breast, and covered her pale face with his tears. But how was he to act? A sudden announcement might startle and distress her.

"There was a Mary Brown," said he, "who was once a housemaid in Mr Peter Ramsay's Inn in St Mary's Wynd."

"And who can it be that can recollect that?" was the answer, as she turned the sightless orbs on the speaker. "Ye maun be full o' years. Yes, that was my happy time, even the only happy time I ever had in this world."

"And there was one William Halket there at that time also," he continued.

Words which, as they fell upon the ear, seemed to be a stimulant so powerful as to produce a jerk in the organ; the dulness of the eyes seemed penetrated with something like light, and a tremor passed over her entire frame.

"That name is no to be mentioned, sir," she said, nervously, "except aince, and nae mair; he was my ruin; for he pledged his troth to me, and promised to come back and marry me, but he never came."

"Nor wrote you?" said Halket.

"No, never," replied she; "I would hae gien the world for a scrape o' the pen o' Will Halket; but it's a' past now, and I fancy he is dead and gone to whaur there is neither plighted troth, nor mar-

F

riage, nor giving in marriage; and my time, too, will be short."

A light broke in upon the mind of Halket, carrying the suspicion that Mr Dreghorn had, for the sake of keeping him at Peach Grove, never forwarded the letters, whereto many circumstances tended.

"And what did you do when you found Will had proved false?" inquired Halket. "Why should that have been your ruin?"

"Because my puir heart was bound up in him," said she, "and I never could look upon another man. Then what could a puir woman do? My mother died, and I came here to work as she wrought: ay, fifty years ago, and my reward has been the puir boon o' the parish bread; ay, and, waur than a' the rest, blindness."

"Mary," said Halket, as he took her emaciated hand into his, scarcely less emaciated, and divested of the genial warmth of life.

The words carried the old sound, and she started and shook.

"Mary!" he continued, "Will Halket still lives. He was betrayed, as you have been betrayed. He wrote three letters to you, all of which were kept back by his master, for fear of losing one who he saw would be useful to him; and, to complete the conspiracy, he reported you dead upon the authority of Peter Ramsay. Whereupon Will betook himself to the making of money, but he never forgot his Mary, whose name has been heard as often as the song of the birds in the groves of Virginia."

"Ah, you are Will himself!" cried she. "I ken now the sound o' your voice in the word 'Mary,' even as you used to whisper it in my ear in the fields at St Leonard's. Let me put my hand upon your head, and move my fingers ower your face. Yes, yes; oh, mercy, merciful God, how can my poor worn heart bear a' this!"

"Mary, my dear Mary!" ejaculated the moved man, "come to my bosom and let me press you to my heart; for this is the only blissful moment I have enjoyed for sixty years."

Nor was Mary deaf to his entreaties, for she resigned herself as in a swoon to an embrace, which an excess of emotion, working on the shrivelled heart and the wasted form, probably prevented her from feeling.

"But, O Willie!" she cried, "a life's love lost; a lost life on both our sides."

"Not altogether," rejoined he, in the midst of their mutual sobs. "It may be—nay, it is—that our sands are nearly run. Yea, a rude shake would empty the glass, so weak and wasted are both of us; but still there are a few grains to pass, and they shall be made golden. You are the only living creature in all this world I have any care for. More thousands of pounds than you ever dreamt of are mine, and will be yours. We will be married even yet, not as the young marry, but as those marry who may look to their knowing each other as husband and wife in heaven, where there are no cruel interested men to keep them asunder; and for the short time we are here you shall ride in your carriage as a lady, and be attended by servants; nor shall a rude breath of wind blow upon you which it is in the power of man to save you from."

"Ower late, Willie; ower late," sighed the exhausted woman, as she still lay in his arms. "But if all this should please my Will—I canna use another name, though you are now a gentleman—I will do even as you list, and that which has been by a cruel fate denied us here we may share in heaven."

"And who shall witness this strange marriage?" said he. "There is no one in Edinburgh now that I know or knows me. Has any one ever been kind to you?"

"Few, few indeed," answered she. "I can count only three."

"I must know these wonderful exceptions," said he, as he made an attempt at a grim smile; " for those who have done a service to Mary Brown have done a double service to me. I will make every shilling they have given you a hundred pounds. Tell me their names."

"There is John Gilmour, my landlord," continued she, "who, though he needed a' his rents for a big family, passed me many a term, and forbye brought me often, when I was ill and couldna work, many a bottle o' wine; there is Mrs Paterson o' the Watergate, too, who aince when I gaed to her in sair need gave me a shilling out o' three that she needed for her bairns; and Mrs Galloway o' Little Lochend, slipt in to me a peck o' meal ae morning when I had naething for breakfast."

"And these shall be at our marriage, Mary," said he. "They shall be dressed to make their eyes doubtful if they are themselves. John Gilmour will wonder how these pounds of his rent he passed you from have grown to hundreds. Mrs Paterson's shilling will have grown as the widow's mite never grew, even in heaven; and Mrs Galloway's peck of meal will be made like the widow's cruse of oil—it will never be finished while she is on earth."

Whereupon Mary raised her head. The blank eyes were turned upon him, and something like a smile played over the thin and wasted face. At the same moment a fair-haired girl of twelve years came jumping into the room, and only stopped when she saw a stranger.

"That is Helen Kemp," said Mary, who knew her movements. "I forgot Helen; she lights my fire, and when I was able to gae out used to lead me to the park."

"And she shall be one of the favoured ones of the earth," said he, as he took by the hand the girl, whom the few words from Mary had made sacred to him, adding, "Helen, dear, you are to be kinder to Mary than you have ever been;" and, slipping into the girl's hand a guinea, he whispered, "You shall have as many of these as will be a bigger tocher to you than you ever dreamed of, for what you have done for Mary Brown."

And thus progressed to a termination a scene perhaps more extraordinary than ever entered into the head of a writer of natural things and events not beyond the sphere of the probable. Nor did what afterwards took place fall short of the intentions of a man whose intense yearnings to make up for what had been lost led him into the extravagance of a vain fancy. He next day took a great house and forthwith furnished it in proportion to his wealth. He hired servants in accordance, and made all the necessary arrangements for the marriage. Time which had been so cruel to him and his sacred Mary was put under the obligation of retribution. John Gilmour, Mrs Paterson, Mrs Galloway, and Helen Kemp were those, and those alone, privileged to witness the ceremony. We would not like to describe how they were decked out, nor shall we try to describe the ceremony itself. But vain are the aspirations of man when he tries to cope with the Fates! The changed fortune was too much for the frail and wasted bride to bear. She swooned at the conclusion of the ceremony, and was put into a silk-curtained bed. Even the first glimpse of grandeur was too much for the spirit whose sigh was vanity, all is vanity, and, with the words on her lips, "A life's love lost," she died.

## The Story of the Merrillygoes.

THE world has been compared to many things,—a playhouse, a madhouse, a penitentiary, a caravanserai, and so forth; but I think a show-box wherein all, including man, is turned by machinery, is better than any of them. And every one looks through his own little round hole at all the rest, he being both object and subject. How the scenes shift too! the belief of one age being the laughing-stock of the next. Witches and brownies and fairies and ghosts and bogles have lost their quiddity, and given birth to quips and laughs; but I have here, as a simple storyteller, to do with one example of these vanished beliefs, what was in folk-lore called the "Merrillygoes," sometimes in the old Scotch dictionaries spelled "Mirrligoes." It was a supposed affection of the eyes, in which the victim or patient, as you suppose the visitation brought on by natural or supernatural powers, fancied he saw men and women and inanimate things which were not at the time before him. I think the affection was different from the "glamour" which was generally attributed to the wrath of fairies; and both indeed might, after all, be resolved into the pseudoblepsy of the old, and the monomania of the new nosologies. But dismissing all learning — which, however potent to puff up man's pride, and then prick the bladder of his conceit, has no concern with a story — I at once introduce to you Mr David Tweedie. He was one of those Davids who, for some Scotch reason, are called Dauvit; and, like other simple men, he had a wife, whose name, I think, was Semple, Robina Semple, certainly not Simple. These worthies figured in Berenger's Close of Edinburgh some time about the provostship of the unfortunate Alexander Wilson; and were not only man and wife by holy Kirk, but a copartnership, insomuch as, Dauvit being a tailor, she after marriage, and having no children to "fash her," became a tailor also, sitting on the same board with him, using the same goose, yea, pricking the same flea with emulous needle.

Yet our couple were in some respects the most unlike each other in the world; Robina being a sharp, clear-witted, nay, ingenious woman — Dauvit a mere big boy. I do not know if I could give the reader a better explanation of the expression I have used than by referring him to the notion he might form of Holbein's picture of his son, whom he quaintly and humorously painted as a man, but retaining all the features, except size, of a boy: the chubby cheeks, small snub nose, pinking eyes, and delicate colours. Nor was Dauvit a big chubby man merely as respected the body, for he was also little better than chubby in mind; at least in so far as regards credulity, passiveness, and softness. He had a marvellous appetite for worldly wonders, the belief being in the direct ratio of the wonderfulness, and he gave credit to the last thing he heard, for no other reason than that it was the last thing; one impression thus effacing another, so that the soft round lump remained always much the same. All which peculiarities were, it may easily be supposed, not only known to, but very well appreciated by, his loving, but perhaps not over-faithful, Binny.

If you keep these things in your mind, you will be able the better to estimate the value of the facts as I proceed to tell you that one morning Dauvit was a little later in getting out of bed than was usual with him, by reason that he had on the previous night been occupied with a suit of those sacredly-imperative things called in Scotland "blacks," that is, mourning. But then the time was not lost; for Robina was up and active, very busily engaged in preparing breakfast. Not that

Dauvit condescended to take much notice of these domestic duties of Binny, because he had ample faith not only in her housewifery, but the wonderful extent of her understanding; only it just happened, as indeed anything *may* happen in a world where we do not know why anything *does* happen, that as he lay very comfortably under the welcome pressure of the soft blankets, with his eyes looking as it were out of a hole, he heard a tap at the door, which tap was just as like that of the letter-carrier as any two blunts of exactly the same length could possibly be. Nor did his observation stop here ; for he saw with these same eyes, as if confirming his ears, Binny go to the door and open it; then came the words of doubtless the said letter-carrier, "That's for Dauvit;" and at the same instant a letter was put into his wife's hands, and thereafter disappeared at the hole of her pocket, where there were many things that David knew nothing about.

Strange as this seemed to Mr Tweedie, even the last act of pocketing would not have appeared to him so very curious if at the moment of secreting the letter she had not very boldly, and even with a kind of smile upon her face, looked fully into the open eyes of her husband. But more still, this sagacious and honest woman immediately thereafter retired into the inner room, where, no doubt, she made herself acquainted with the contents of the communication, whatever it might be, and from which she came again to resume, as she did resume, her preparations for breakfast just as if nothing had happened beyond what was common. Of course I need not say that Dauvit was astonished; but his astonishment was an increasing quantity in proportion to the time that now passed without her going forward to the bedside and reading the letter to him, as she had often done before; and if we might be entitled to wonder why he didn't at once put the question, "What letter was that, Binny?" perhaps the answer which would have been given by David himself might have been that his very wonder prevented him from asking for an explanation of the wonder—just as miracles shut people's mouths at the same moment that they make them open their eyes.

However this might be—and who knows but that David might have a pawky curiosity to try Binny?—the never a word did he say; but, rising slowly and quietly, he dressed himself, in that loose way in which of all tradesmen the tailors most excel, for a reason of which I am entirely ignorant. He then sat down by the fire; and Binny having seated herself on the other side, the operation of breakfast began without a word being said on either part, but with mutual looks, which on the one side, viz., Robina's, were very well understood, but on the other not at all. A piece of pantomime all this which could not last very long, for the good reason that impatience is the handmaiden of curiosity; and David at length, in spite of a bit of bread which almost closed up his mouth, got out the words—

"What letter was that, Binny, which the letter-carrier handed in this mornin'?"

"Letter! there was nae letter, man," was the answer of Binny, accompanied with a look of surprise, which might in vain compete with the wonder immediately called up in the eyes of her simple husband.

"Did I no see it with my ain cen?" was the very natural ejaculation.

"No, you didn't; you only thought ye saw it," said the wife; "and thae twa things have a gey difference between them."

"What *do* ye mean, Robina, woman?"

"The merrillygoes!"

"The merrillygoes," rejoined the wondering David; "my cen niver were in that condition."

"*You* may think sae, Dauvit," rejoined Binny; "but I happen to ken better. On Wednesday night, when we were in bed, and the moon shining in at the window, did I no hear you say, 'Binny, woman, what are ye doing up at this eery hour?' It was just about twelve; and upon lifting my head and looking ower at ye, I saw your een staring out as gleg as a hawk's after a sparrow. It had begun then."

"Ou, I had been dreaming," said David.

"Dreaming with your een open!"

"That is indeed strange enough," rejoined David. "Did ye really see my een open?"

"Did ye ever hear me tell ye a lee, man? Am I no as true as the Bible? and think ye I dinna ken the strange light o' the merrillygoes, when I have seen it in the een o' my ain father?"

"Is that really true, Binny? I'm beginnin' to get fear'd. But what o' your father, lass?"

"Ye may weel ask," said the wife. "He had been awa' at Falkirk Tryst with his ewes, and it was about seven o'clock when he cam' hame. We were then in the farm o' Kimmergame. Weel, he was coming up the lang loan, and it was gloaming; and just when he was about twenty yards from his ain door, he saw twa men hurrying along with a coffin a' studded with white nails. They were only a yard or twa before him, and the moment he saw them he stopped till he saw where they were going; and yet where could they be going but to his ain house; and nae doubt his wife would be dead, for the lang coffin couldna have fitted any other person in the house; but he was soon made sure enough, for he saw the men with the coffin enter into his ain door, and there he stood in a swither o' fear; but he was a brave man, and in he went, never stopping till he got into his ain parlour, where my mother was sitting at her tea, and nae sooner did she see him than she broke out in a laugh o' perfect joy at his hamecome. But the never a word he ever said about the coffin, because he didn't wish to terrify his wife with evil omens; and besides, he understood the vision perfectly. And, Dauvit, if ye're a wise man ye will submit to the hand o' God, wha sees fit to bring thae visitations upon us for some wise end."

"Very true," said David, to whom the affair of the letter was rather much even for *his* credulity; "but still, Binny, lass, I canna just come to it that I was deceived."

"Weel, weel, stick to it, my man, and mak me, your ain wife, a lecar."

"That canna be either," rejoined David; "and by my faith, I'm at a loss what to think or what to do; for if it really be that the infliction's upon me, how, in the Lord's name, am I to ken the real thing from the fause? My head rins right round at the very thought o't. And then I fancy there's nae remedy in the power o' man."

"I fear no," replied Binny. "Ye maun just pray; but I have heard my father say that it came on him after he had been confined with an ill-working stomach to the house, and exercise drove it away. Ye've been sitting ower close. Take scouth for a day. Awa' ower to Burntisland, and get payment from John Sprunt o' the three pounds he owes for his last suit. Stay ower the night. I say nothing about the jolly boose ye'll have thegither, but it may drive thae fumes and fancies out o' your head. Come ower with the first boat in the morning, and I will have your breakfast ready for you."

The prudence of this advice David was not slow to see, though he had, maugre his simplicity, considerable misgivings about the affair of the letter; nor did he altogether feel the absolute conviction that he was under the influence of the foresaid mysterious power. But independently of the prudence of her counsel, he felt it as a command, and therefore behoved to obey. For we may as well admit that David might doubt of the eternal obligation of a certain decalogue by reason of its being abrogated; but as for the commands of Mrs Robina, they were subject to no abrogation, and certainly no denial whatever. So David went and dressed himself in his "second-best"—a particular mentioned here with an after-view — and having got from the hands of her, who was thus both wife and medical adviser, a drop of spirits to help him *on*, and the merrillygoes *off*, he set forth on his journey.

Proceeding down Leith Wynd, he found himself in Leith Walk; but however active his limbs, thus relieved on so short a warning from "the board," and however keen and far-sighted his eyes, as they scanned all the people he met, he could not shake off certain doubts whether the individuals he met were in reality creatures of flesh and blood, or mere visions. The sacred words of Mrs Robina were a kind of winged beliefs, which, by merely striking on the ear, performed for him what many a man has much trouble in doing for himself— that is, thinking; so that upon the whole the tendency of his thoughts was in a great degree favourable to sadness and terror. The sigh was heaved again and again; being sometimes for a longer period delayed, as the hope of a jolly boose with his friend Sprunt held a partial sway in his troubled mind. But by and by the activity required by his search for a boat, the getting on board, the novelty of the sail, the undulating movements, and all the interests which belong to a "traveller by sea and land," drove away the cobwebs that hung about the brain; and by the time he got to Burntisland he was much as he used to be. But, alas, he little knew that this journey, propitious as it appeared,

G

was not calculated to produce the wonderful effects expected from it.

No sooner had he landed on the pier than he made straight for the house of his friend, which stood by the roadside, a little removed from the village. He saw it in the distance; and quickening his steps, came to an angle which enabled him to see into Mr Sprunt's garden; and we may, considering how much the three pounds, the boose, the fun, the cure was associated with the figure of that individual, imagine the satisfaction felt by Mr Tweedie when he saw the true body of John Sprunt in that very garden, busily engaged, too, in the delightful occupation of garden-work, and animated, we may add of our own supposition, with a mind totally oblivious of the three pounds he owed to the Edinburgh tailor. But well and truly may we speak of the uncertainty of mundane things. David had only turned away his eyes for an instant, and yet in that short period, as he found when he again turned his head, the well-known figure of his old friend, pot-companion, and debtor in three pounds, had totally disappeared. The thing looked like what learned people call a phenomenon. How could Sprunt have disappeared so soon? Where could he have gone to be invisible, where there was no summer-house to receive him, and where the time did not permit of a retreat into his own dwelling? David stood, and began to think of the words of Robina. There could be no doubt that his eyes had been at fault again; it was not John Sprunt he had seen—merely a lying image. And so even on the instant the old sadness came over him again, with more than one long sigh; nor in his depression and simplicity was he able to bring up any such recondite thing as a thought suggesting the connexion between John's disappearance and the fact that he owed Mr David Tweedie—whom he could have seen in the road—the sum of three pounds.

In which depressed and surely uncomfortable condition our traveller proceeded towards the house, more anxious, indeed, to disprove his terrors than to get his money. He knocked at the door, which, by the by, was at the end of the house; and his knock was answered by Mrs Sprunt herself, a woman who could have acted Bellona in an old Greek piece.

"I am glad John is at hame," were David's first words.

"And I would be glad if that were true, Mr Dauvit," replied she; "but it just happens no to be true. John went off to Kirkaldy at six o'clock this morning to try and get some siller that's due him there."

"Let me in to sit down," muttered David, with a kind of choking in his voice.

And following the good dame into the parlour, Mr Tweedie threw himself into the arm-chair in a condition of great fear and perturbation. Having sat mute for a minute or two, probably to the wonderment of the dame, he began to rub his brow with his handkerchief, as if taking off a little perspiration could help him in his distress.

"Mrs Sprunt," said he, "I could have sworn that I saw John working in the yard."

Whereat Mrs Sprunt broke out into a loud laugh, which somehow or another seemed to David as ghostly as his visions; and when she had finished she added, "Something wrong, Dauvit, with your een."

"Gudeness gracious and ungracious!" said David. "Is this possible? Can it really be? Whaur, in the name o' Heeven, am I to look for a real flesh-and-blood certainty?"

"And yet ye seem to be sober, Dauvit."

"As a judge," replied he. But, after a pause, "Can I be sure even o' *you?*" he cried, as he started up; the while his eyes rolled in a manner altogether very unlike the douce quiet character he bore. "Let me satisfy mysel that you are really Mrs Janet Sprunt in the real body."

And making a sudden movement, with his arms

extended towards the woman, he tried to grip her; but it was a mere futile effort. Mrs Sprunt was gone through the open door in an instant, and David was left alone with another confirmation of his dreaded suspicion, muttering to himself, " There too, there too,—a' alike; may the Lord have mercy upon His afflicted servant! Robina Tweedie, ye were right after a', and that letter was a delusion like the rest—a mere eemage—a' eemages thegither."

After which soliloquy he again sat down in the easy-chair, held his hands to his face, and groaned in the pain of a wounded spirit. But even in the midst of this solemn conviction that the Lord had laid His hand upon him, he could see that sitting there could do him no good; and, rising up, he made for the kitchen. There was no one there; he tried another room, which he also found empty; and issuing forth from the unlucky house, he encountered an old witch-looking woman who was turning the corner, as if going in the direction of another dwelling.

" Did you see Mrs Sprunt even now?" said he.

" No likely," answered the woman; " when she tauld me this mornin' she was going to Petticur. She has a daughter there, ye ken."

Melancholy intelligence which seemed to have a logical consistency with the other parts of that day's remarkable experiences; nor did David seem to think that anything more was necessary for the entire satisfaction of even a man considerably sceptical, and then who in those days doubted the merrillygoes?

"What poor creatures we are!" said he. "I came here for a perfect cure, and I gae hame with a heavy care."

And with these words, which were in reality an articulated groan, Mr David Tweedie made his way back towards the pier, under an apprehension that as he went along he would meet with some verification of a suspicion which, having already become a conviction, not only required no more proof, but was strong enough to battle all opposing facts and arguments; so he went along with his chin upon his breast, and his eyes fixed upon the ground, as if he were afraid to trust them with a survey of living beings, lest they might cheat him as they had already done. It was about half-past twelve when he got to the boat; and he was further disconcerted by finding that the wind, which had brought him so cleverly over, would repay itself, like over-generous givers, who take back by one hand what they give by the other. And so it turned out; for he was fully two hours on the passage, all of which time was occupied by a reverie as to the extraordinary calamity that had befallen him. And how much more dreary his cogitations as he thought of the increased unhappiness of Robina, when she ascertained not only the failure of getting payment of his debt, but the total wreck of her means of cure!

At length he got to Leith pier; but his landing gave him no pleasure: he was still haunted with the notion that he would encounter more mischances; and he hurried up Leith Walk, passing old friends whom he was afraid to speak to. Arrived at the foot of Leith Wynd, he made a detour which brought him to the foot of Halkerston's Wynd, up which he ascended, debouching into the High Street. And here our story becomes so incredible, that we are almost afraid to trust our faithful pen to write what David Tweedie saw on his emerging from the entry. There, coming up the High Street, was Mrs Robina Tweedie herself, marching along steadily, dressed in David's best suit. He stood and stared with goggle eyes, as if he felt some strange pleasure in the fascination. The vision was so concrete, that he could identify his own green coat made by his own artistic fingers. There were the white metal buttons, the broadest he could get in the whole city—nay, one of them on the back had been scarcely a match, and he recognised the defect; his knee-breeches too, so easily detected by their having been made out of a large remnant of a colour (purple) whereof there was not another bit either to be bought or "cabbaged,"—nay, the very brass knee-buckles of which he was so proud; the "rig-and-fur" stockings of dark brown; the shoe-buckles furbished up the last Sunday; the square hat he had bought from Pringle; and, to crown all, his walking-stick with the ivory top. So perfect indeed was the "get-up" of his lying eyes, that, if he had not been under the saddening impression of his great visitation, he would have been well amused by the wonderful delusion. Even as it was, he could not help following the phantom, as it went so proudly and jantily along the street. And what was still more extraordinary, he saw Mucklewham, the city guardsman, meet her and speak to her in a private kind of way, and then go away with her. But David had a trace of sense in his soft nature. He saw that it was vain as well as hurtful to gratify what was so clearly a delusion; it would only deepen the false images in eyes already sufficiently "glamoured;" and so he stopped suddenly short and let them go—that is, he would cease *to look*,—and they, the visions, would cease *to be*. In all which how little did he know that he was prefiguring a philosophy which was some time afterwards to become so famous! Nay, are we not all under the merrillygoes in this world of phantoms?

> "You say you see the things that be:
> I say you only think you see.
> Not even that. It seems to me
> You only think you think you see.
> Then thinking weaves so many a lie,
> Methinks this world is 'all my eye.'"

But even in his grief and sacred fear he could not help saying to himself, "Gude Lord! if that eemage werena frightfu', would it no be funny? And what will Robina say? Nae doubt she is at this very moment sitting at her tea in Berenger's Close, thinking upon my calamity. What *will* she say when I tell her that I saw her in the High Street dressed in my Sunday suit, walking just as if she were Provost Wilson himsel? I wouldna wonder if she should get into ane o' her laughing fits, even in very spite o' her grief for the awful condition of her loving husband. At any rate, it's time I were hame, when I canna tell what I am to see next, nor can even say which end o' me is uppermost."

Nor scarcely had he finished his characteristic soliloquy, when a hand was laid on his shoulder. It was that of the corporal; but how was David to know that? Why, he felt Bill's hand; and to make things more certain, he even laid his own hand upon the solid shoulder of the sturdy city guardsman; adding, for still greater proof—

"Did you meet and speak to any one up the street there?"

"The niver a living soul," said the corporal, "as I'm a sinner; but come along, man, to the Prophet Amos's," (a well-known tavern in the Canongate,) "and let us have a jolly jug, for I'm to be on duty to-night, and need something to cheer me up; and the colour of ale will sit better on your cheeks when you go home to Robina than that saffron. Are you well enough, David? I think I might as well ask the question of a half-hanged dog."

"Half or hale hanged," replied David, as he eyed his friend suspiciously, "I canna be the waur o' a jug o' ale."

An answer which was perhaps the result of sheer despair, for the conviction of the "real unreality" of what he had seen was now so much beyond doubt that he began to submit to it as a doom; and what is irremediable becomes, like death, to be bearable, nay, even accommodating to the routine of life; and so the two jogged along till they came to the Prophet's, where they sat down to their liquor and, we may add, loquacity, of which latter Mucklewham was so profuse, that any other less simple person than David might have thought that the guardsman wanted to speak against time. But David suspected nothing, and he was the more inclined to be patient that his friend had promised to pay the score.

"And when saw ye Robina?" said David.

"Not for a good round year, my bairn," said the big corporal.

"Gude Lord, did ye no see her and speak to her even this day?"

Whereupon the big guardsman laughed a horse (guardsman's) laugh; and pointing his finger to his eye he twirled the same, that is the finger, merrily round. A movement which David too well understood; and after heaving a deep sigh, he took a deep pull at the ale, as if in a paroxysm of despair.

And so they drank on, till David having risen and left the room for a breath of fresh air, found on his return that his generous friend had vanished. Very wonderful, no doubt. But, then, had he not taken his jug with him?—no doubt to get it replenished—and he would return with a filled tankard. Vain expectation! Mucklewham was only another Sprunt, another lie of the visual sense. Did David Tweedie really need this new proof? David knew he didn't; neither did he require the additional certainty of his calamity by having to pay only for his own "shot." The Prophet did not ask for more, nor did he think it necessary to say why; perhaps he would make the corporal pay his own share afterwards. The whole thing was as clear as noon: David had been drinking with one who had no stomach wherein to put his liquor, and for the good reason that he had no body to hold that stomach.

"Waur than the case o' the letter, or Sprunt, (hiccup,) or Robina dressed in my claes," said he lugubriously, "for I only *saw* them, but I handled the corporal, sat with him, drank with him, heard him speak; yet baith he and the pewter jug were off in a moment, and I hae paid (hic) only for ae man's drink. But is it no a' a dream thegither? I wouldna wonder I am at this very moment in my bed wi' Robina lying at my back."

And rising up, he discovered that he was not very well able to keep his legs, the more by reason that he had poured the ale into an empty stomach; there was, besides, a new confusion in his brain, as if that organ had not already enough to do with any small powers of maintaining itself in equilibrium which it possessed. But he behoved to get home; and to Berenger's Close he accordingly went, making sure as he progressed of at least one truth in nature, amidst all the dubieties and delusions of that most eventful day: that the shortest way between two points is the deflecting one. And what was Binny about when he entered his own house? Working the button-holes of a vest which had been left by David unfinished. No sooner did she see David staggering in than she threw the work aside.

"Hame already? and in that state too!" she cried. "You must have been seeing strange ferlies in the High Street, while I was sitting here busy at my wark."

"Strange enough, lass; but if you can tell me whether or no I am Dauvit Tweedie, your lawfu' husband or the Prophet Moses, or the Apostle Aaron, or (hic) the disciple Deuteronomy, or the deevil, it's mair than I can."

Whereupon David dropt his uncertain body in a chair, doubting perhaps if even the chair was really a chair.

"And it was na just enough," rejoined she, "that you had an attack of the merrillygoes, but you must add pints o' ale to make your poor wits mair confounded."

A remark which Robina thought herself entitled to make, irrespective of the question which for a hundred years has been disputed, viz., whether she had sent the corporal to take David to Prophet Amos's and fill him drunk with ale, and then shirk the score?

"But haste ye to bed, my man," she added, "that's the place for you, where you may snore awa' the fumes o' Prophet Amos's ale, and the whimwhams o' your addled brain."

An advice which David took kindly, though he did not need it; for, educated as he may be said to have been by the clever Robina, he was fortunately one of those favoured beings pointed at in the wise saying that the power of education is seldom effectual except in those happy cases where it is superfluous. So it was the ale that sent him to bed and to sleep as well—a condition into which he sunk very soon. And it was kindly granted to him, insomuch as it was a kind of recompense for what he had suffered during that day of wonders: it saved him from the possibility of hearing a conversation in the other room between Robina and the corporal, in the course of which it was asked and answered whether David had recognised Robina in her male decorations; and whether he had any suspicions as to the true character of the deep plot they were engaged in working out.

What further took place in the house of Mr Tweedie that night we have not been able, notwithstanding adequate inquiry, to ascertain; but of this important fact we are well assured, that next morning David awoke in a much improved condition. To account for this we must remember his peculiar nature, for to him "the yesterday," whatever yesterday it might be, was always a *dies non;* it had done its duty and was gone, and it had no business here any more than an impudent fellow who tries to live too long after the world is sick of him. Indeed, we know that he ate such a breakfast, and with such satisfaction, that no ideas of a yesterday had any chance of resisting the feelings of the moment; and once gone, they had too much difficulty to get into the dark chamber again to think of trying it. He was "on the board" by ten o'clock. For he had work to do, and as Robina's purpose was in the meantime served, she said no more of the merrillygoes. She had perhaps something else to do; for shortly after eleven she went out, perhaps to report to the corporal the sequel to that which he already knew. But whatever her object, her absence was not destined to be so fruitful of good to her as her presence wherever she might go; for it so happened that as David was sitting working, and sometimes with his face overcast with a passing terror of a return of his calamity, he found he required a piece of cloth of a size and colour whereof there were some specimens in an old trunk. To that repository of cabbage, as it is vulgarly called, he went; and in rummaging through the piebald contents he came upon a parcel in a corner. On opening it, he found to his great wonderment no fewer than a hundred guineas of pure gold. The rays from the shiny pieces seemed to enter his eyes like spikes, and fix the balls in the sockets; if he felt a kind of fascination yesterday as he looked at his wife in male attire, though a mere vision, he experienced the influence now even more, however doubtful he was of the reality of the glittering objects. He seized, he clutched them, he shut his eyes, and opened them again as he opened his hands; they did *not* disappear; but then Robina herself might appear, and under this apprehension, which put to flight his doubts, he carried them off, and secreted them in a private drawer of which he had the key; whereupon he betook himself again to the board. By and by Robina returned; but the never a word David said of the guineas, because he had still doubts of the veracity of his eyes.

And so the day passed without anything occurring to suggest either inquiry or answer. During the night David slept so soundly that he was even oblivious of his prize; and it was not till eleven next forenoon, when his wife went out, that he ventured to look into the drawer; but now the terrible truth was revealed to him: the guineas were gone, and he had been again under delusion. The merrillygoes once more! and how was he to admit the fact to Robina, after his attempted appropriation!

But, happily, there was no necessity for admitting his own shame, for about four o'clock John Jardine the letter-carrier called and told him that his wife had eloped with the corporal. The intelligence was no doubt very dreadful to David, who loved his wife so dearly that he could have subscribed to the saying "that the husband will always be deceived when the wife condescends to dissemble;" but Mrs Robina Tweedie did not so condescend; and David now began to see certain things and to recollect certain circumstances which, when put together, appeared even to his mind more strange than the merrillygoes. And his eyes were opened still further by a letter from Kirkcudbright from a Mr Gordon, wishing to be informed why he had not acknowledged the receipt of the hundred guineas left him by his uncle, and which had been sent in a prior letter in the form of a draft on the Bank of Scotland. Mr David Tweedie now went to the bank, and was told that the money had been paid to a man in a green coat and white metal buttons, square hat, and walking-stick, who represented himself as David Tweedie.

Our story, it will be seen, has pretty nearly explained itself; yet something remains to be told. A whole year elapsed, when one morning Mrs Robina Tweedie appeared before honest David, with a lugubrious face and a lugubrious tale, to the effect that although she had been tempted to run away with the corporal, she had almost immediately left him — a pure, bright, unsullied wife; but during all this intermediate time she had felt so ashamed and conscience-stricken, that she could not return and ask forgiveness. All which David heard, and to all which he answered—

"Robina—nae mair Tweedie, lass—ye ken I was afflicted with a strange calamity when ye left me. I thought I saw what wasna to be seen. It comes aye back upon me now and then; and I ken it's on me this mornin'. I may think I see you there standin' before me, even as I saw you in my broad-tailed coat that day in the High Street; but I ken it's a' a delusion. In fact, my dear Robina, *I dinna see you, I dinna even feel your body,*" (pushing her out by the cuff of the neck;) "the merrillygoes, lass! the merrillygoes!"

And David shut the door on the ejected Robina—thereafter living a very quiet and comparatively happy life, free from all glamour or any other affection of the eyes, and seeing just as other people see. Yea, with his old friend Sprunt and his wife he had many a joke on the subject, forgiving John for running away that morning to shirk his creditor, as well as Mrs Janet for being terrified out of the house by the wild rolling eyes of the unhappy David.

## The Story of the Six Toes.

A MAN who makes a will generally knows pretty well the person to whom he leaves a legacy, but it does not follow that other people are to have the same enlightenment as to the identity of the legatee. I make the remark in reference to a common story connected with the will of honest Andrew Gebbie, who officiated once as a ruling elder in the Church of Trinity College, Edinburgh, and was supposed to have done so much good to the people by his prayers, exhortations and psalm-singing, that it was utterly unnecessary for his getting to heaven, where he had sent so many others, that he should bequeath a single plack or bawbee to the poor when he died. Yet whether it was that the good man Andrew determined to make sure work of his salvation, or that he had any less ambitious object in view, certain it is that some time before he died he made a will by his own hand, and without the help of a man of the law, in spite of the Scotch adage—

> "Who saves a fee and writes his will
> Is friendly to the lawyers still;
> For these take all the will contains,
> And give the heir all that remains."

And by this said will honest Andrew bequeathed the sum of three hundred pounds sterling money to "Mistress Helen Grey, residing in that street of the old town called Leith Wynd," without any further identification or particularisation whatsoever, nor did he say a single word about the cause of making this somewhat generous bequest, or anything about the merits or services of the legatee. A strange circumstance, seeing that the individual being a "Nelly Grey" had long been a favourite of the poets, (and, therefore, rather indefinite,) as she indeed still figures in more than one very popular song, wherein she is even called bonny Nelly Grey.

Then, to keep all matters in harmony, he appointed three clergymen—the minister of his own church, the minister of the Tolbooth, and the minister of the Tron—as his executors for carrying his said will into execution, probably thinking that Nelly Grey's three hundred, and her soul to boot, could not be in better hands than those of such godly men. So, after living three weeks longer in a very bad world, the worthy testator was gathered to his fathers, and it might perhaps have been as well that his said will had been gathered along with him,—as indeed happened in a recent case, where a sensible man, probably in fear of the lawyers, got his will placed in the same coffin with him,—though no doubt he forgot that worms, if not moths, do corrupt there also, and sometimes thieves, in the shape of body-snatchers, do break through and steal. Passing all which we proceed to say that the executors entered upon their duties. As regards the other legatees they found no difficulty whatever, most probably because legatees are a kind of persons who are seldom out of the way when they are wanted. They accordingly made their appearance, and without a smile, which would have been unbecoming, got payment of their legacies. But as for this Helen Grey, with so large a sum standing at her credit, she made no token of any kind, nor did any of the relations know aught concerning her, though they wondered exceedingly who she could be, and how she came to be in so strange a place as their kinsman's testament. Not that the three executors, the ministers, shared very deeply in this wondering, because they knew that their elder, honest Andrew, was a good and godly man, and had had good and godly, and therefore sufficient reasons, (probably in the poverty and piety of Helen,) for doing what he had done.

If indeed these gentlemen wondered at all, it was simply that any poor person living in such a place as Leith Wynd should be so regardless of money, as to fail to make her appearance among the grave and happy legatees. The question, who can she be, passed from the one to the other like a bad shilling. Not one of them could answer. Father Tron, and Father Tolbooth, and Father Trinity, were all at fault; the noses of their ingenuity could not smell out the object of their wish. But then they had been trusting so far as yet to the relatives, and had not made personal inquiry in Leith Wynd, which, if they had been men of business, they would have done at once.

"Oh," said Father Trinity at length, "I think I have it now when I recollect there was an honest woman of that name who was a member of my congregation some years ago, and, if I am not mistaken, she was in honest Andrew Gebbie's visiting district, and he took an interest in her soul."

"The thing is patent," rejoined Father Tron. "Our lamented elder hath done this good thing out of the holy charity that cometh of piety."

"And a most beautiful example of the fruits of godliness," added Father Tolbooth.

"Beautiful indeed!" said Trinity. "For we have here to keep in view that Elder Andrew had many poor friends, but he hath chosen to prefer the relationship of the spirit to that of mere earthly connexion. And his reward will verily be reaped in heaven."

"We must give the good man a paragraph in the *Mercury*," resumed Father Tolbooth. "And now, brother of Trinity, it will be for you to find Helen Grey out, and carry to her the glad tidings."

"A pleasant commission," rejoined Father Trinity, as he rose to depart.

And taking his way to Leith Wynd, he soon reached that celebrated street, nor was it long till he passed "The Happy Land," that dreaded den of burglars, thieves, and profligate women, which the Scotch, according to their peculiar humour, had so named. That large building he behoved to pass with a sigh as the great forlorn hope of the city, and coming to some of the brokers whose shops were farther down, he procured some information which sent him up a dark close, to the end of which having got, he ascended to a garret in a back tenement, and, knocking at the door, was answered by an aged woman.

"Does Helen Grey live here?"

"Ay, sir!" replied she. "If ye ca' living the breathing awa o' the breath o' life. It's a sad thing when auld age and poverty come thegither."

"An old saying, Helen," replied the father.

"Yet there is a third one which sanctifieth the other two, and bringeth all into harmony, peace, and love, and that is religion. But do you not know your old minister?"

"Brawly, brawly, sir," replied she; "but the truth is, I didna like to speak first; and now, sir, I'm as proud as if I had got a fortune."

"And so perhaps you have," added the father. "But come, sit down. I've got something to say;" and having seated himself he continued. "Was Maister Andrew Gebbie, our worthy elder, in the habit of visiting you?"

"Indeed, and he did aince or twice come and see me; but never mair," replied she. "Yet he was sae kind as to bring me the last time this book o' psalms and paraphrases, and there's some writing in 't which I couldna read."

"Let me see it," he said.

And the woman having handed him the book—

"To Mrs Janet Grey," said the minister, as he read the inscription.

"A mistake, for my name is Helen," said she. "But it was weel meant in Mr Gebbie, and it's a' the same."

"A staff to help her on to the happy land," continued the reverend doctor, reading.

"No 'The Happy Land' near bye?" interjected Helen.

"Not likely," continued the doctor with a smile. "But I have good news for you, Helen."

"Good news for me!" said the woman. "That must come frae an airth no within the four quarters o' the earthly compass. I thought a' gude news for *me* had ta'en wings, and floun awa to the young and the happy."

"It seems not,' said he; "for Elder Andrew has left you a legacy of three hundred pounds."

"Stop, stop, sir!" ejaculated the frightened legatee. "It canna be, and though it was sae, I couldna bear the grandeur. It would put out the sma' spark o' life that's left in my auld heart."

"No, no!" said he. "It is only an earthly inheritance, Helen, to keep you in ease and comfort in your declining years, till you succeed to that inheritance which knoweth no decay, and fadeth not away."

"But is it really possible, good sir?" she continued, a little reconciled to that whereunto there is a pretty natural predisposition in human nature. "But I havena blessed Elder Andrew yet. May the Lord receive Andrew Gebbie's soul into endless glory!"

"Amen!" said the reverend doctor. "I will speak of this again to you, Helen."

And with these words he left the still confused woman, who would very likely still feel a difficulty in comprehending the length and breadth of the goodness of a man who had seen her only a few times, and given her a psalm-book, and called her Janet in place of Helen—a mistake he must have rectified before he made his will.

Next day the reverend doctor of Trinity had another meeting in the office of the law-agent to the trust, Mr George Crawford, whereat he recounted how he had found out the legatee; how strange it was that the poor woman was entirely ignorant of her good fortune; how grateful she was; and, above all, how strange that the saintly elder had only seen her a few times, and knew so little of her that he had made the foresaid mistake in her name. All which did seem strange to the brethren, not any one of whom would even have thought of giving more than perhaps a pound to such a person. But as the motives of men are hidden from the eyes of their fellows, and are indeed like the skins of onions, placed one above another, so they considered that all they had to do was to walk by the will.

"We have no alternative," said Father Tron; "nor should we wish any, seeing that the money could not be better applied; for has not the son of Sirach said, 'Give unto a godly man, and not unto a sinner.'"

"And," added Tolbooth, "we are also commanded to give of our substance to the poor, and 'do well unto those that are lowly.'"

"Yes," said Father Trinity. "Mr Gebbie's object was clear enough; it was sufficient for him that the woman was poor; therein lay his reward; and I presume we have nothing to do but to authorise Mr Crawford to pay the money."

"Which I will do, gentlemen," said the writer, "if you authorise me; but I frankly confess to you that I am not altogether satisfied, because I knew Mr Andrew Gebbie intimately, and, godly as he was, I can hardly think he was the man to make a comparative stranger the medium of the accumulation of compound interest to be got back in heaven. Besides, Helen Grey is so common a name, that I believe I could get several in Edinburgh; and if we were to pay to the wrong woman, you might be bound to refund out of your own stipends, which would not be a very pleasant thing."

A speech which, touching the word stipend, brought a very grave look into the faces of the brethren.

"A most serious, yea, a momentous consideration," said Tron, followed by the two others.

Nor had the groan got time to die away when the door opened, and there stood before them a woman of somewhere about forty, a little shabby in her apparel, though with a decayed flush of gaudy colour in it here and there; somewhat blowsy too—the tendency to the tint of the peony being more evident about the region of the nose, where there was a spot or two very clearly predisposed to the sending forth, under favourable circumstances, of a pimple; rather bold-looking in addition, even in presence of holy men who wielded the Calvinistic thunders of the day, and followed them up with the refreshing showers of grace and love.

"I understand," said she, "that Elder Andrew Gebbie has left me a legacy o' three hundred pounds, and I will thank you for the siller."

On hearing which the three fathers looked at each other in amazement, and it was clear they did not like the appearance of the new claimant.

"Who are you?" said Trinity.

"Helen Grey!" replied she. "I live in Leith Wynd. Mr Andrew Gebbie and me were man and wife."

"Where are your marriage lines?" asked Tron.

"I hae nane," replied she. "It was a marriage by giving and taking between ourselves—a gude marriage by the law."

"And no witnesses?" said Tron.

"The deil ane but the Lord."

"Wh-e-w!" whistled Father Tron, not audibly, only as it were within the mouth.

"It is very true," said Father Trinity, as he looked askance at the claimant, and contrasted her in his mind with the other Nelly, who he was satisfied was the real Nelly Pure, "that Mr Andrew Gebbie left that sum of money to a certain Helen Grey, but we have no evidence to show that you are the right woman."

"The right woman!" ejaculated she, with a bold laugh; "and how could I be the wrong ane, when I cut Andrew Gebbie's corns for ten years?"

"Oh, a chiropodist!" said Father Tron.

"I'm nae corn-doctor, sir," replied she, with something like offended pride: "I never cut another man's corns in my life."

"We are nearly getting into that lightness of speech which betokeneth vanity," said another of the brethren. "It is a serious matter; and we must require of you, Mrs Grey—seeing that the marriage cannot, even by your own statement, be taken into account, for want of evidence—to prove that you were upon such terms of friendship with Mr Gebbie as to make it probable that he would leave you this large sum of money."

"Friendship!" cried the woman again. "Ay, for ten years, and wha can tell where the flee may stang? It was nae mair than he should have dune. I am Helen Grey, and I insist upon my rights."

"But," said Father Trinity, "there is another Helen Grey in Leith Wynd, with whom Mr Gebbie was acquainted, and to whom he made a present of a psalm-book."

"And did he no gie me a psalm-book too!" quoth the woman. "I have it at hame, and you are welcome to see my name on't written by the elder's ain hand. But did this second Helen Grey cut the good elder's corns for ten lang years, I wonder? Tell me that, gentlemen, and I'll tell you something mair that will make your ears ring as they never did at a psalm."

"Still this irreverend nonsense about corns: woman, are you mad?" said Tron. "Give us the names of respectable people who knew of this asserted friendship between you and the deceased elder."

"The deil ane kent o't, sir, but ourselves!" was the sharp answer of the woman. "And if it comes to that, I can prove naething; but I tell you there's mair in the corns than ye wot."

"Oh! she wants to prove the *footing* she was on with Mr Gebbie," punned Mr Crawford with a laugh, and the grave brethren could not help joining in what Tron called a fine example of the figure called *paronomasia*.

"That's just it," said the woman. "I will prove that I knew the length o' his big tae, and may be mair."

"And what more?" asked Father Tron.

"That Mr Gebbie had six toes on his left foot!" answered she.

"And what of that?" inquired the agent, as he pricked up his ears at what might turn out a more special means of knowledge than they were dreaming of.

"A great deal," continued the woman. "Sae muckle that I need nae mair, for be it kenned to ye that Mr Gebbie was aye ashamed o' what he thought a deformity, and concealed it from a' living mortals except me. If ye'll prove that there's anither person in a' Edinburgh, in Scotland, or in the hail world, wha kens that Elder Andrew had six toes on his left foot, I'll give up a' right to the three hundred pounds!"

"So there is something in the corns after all," whispered Mr Crawford to Trinity, and the others hearing the remark began to think, and think, and look at each other, as if they felt that the woman had fairly shut them up to a test of her truthfulness easily applied. So telling her to call back next day at the same hour, they requested her to leave them. And after she was gone, the four gentlemen began gradually to relax from their gravity as they saw the ingenuity of the woman, for it was quite apparent that if it should turn out that no one—servant, relative, or doctor—could tell this wonderful fact about the six toes of their own knowledge, however derived, and that this Helen Grey was the sole confidential custodier thereof—the conclusion was all but certain that she knew it by being intrusted with the cutting of the holy man's corns, as she had asserted. And a confidence of this kind, (setting aside the irregular marriage,) implied a friendship so close as to justify the legacy. What in the meantime remained to be done was for the agent to see any persons connected with the elder's household who were likely to know the fact, and being an honourable man he behoved to do this without what is called a leading question.

Accordingly, that same afternoon Mr Crawford busied himself to the effect of having seen the good elder's housekeeper, as well as the doctor who had attended him upon his last illness, with perhaps a dozen of other likely people, such as the other legatees and relations, all of whom were entirely ignorant of the fact set forth by the woman, viz., that Mr Gebbie had six toes on his left foot. And next day the trustees met again, when Mr Crawford told them, before touching on the corns, that an agent had called upon him from the other

Helen first seen, demanding payment to her. He then told the trustees the result of his inquiries—that not a single person of all he had seen knew anything of the abnormal foot. At this the clergymen wondered more and more, and how long they might have sat there and wondered it might have been difficult to say, had it not been for an ingenious idea started by Tron, and suggested by the old story about King Charles and the fish in the bucket of water.

"The woman is laughing at us," said he, "and we are inquiring whether certain people knew a fact without making ourselves acquainted with the prior fact, whether that prior fact had ever any existence except in the brain of this bad woman, whose evidence goes to traduce the character of a holy elder of the Church of Scotland."

The brethren again laughed at this ingenious discovery of Father Tron's, and thereupon began to veer round in favour of good Nelly *prima*. In a few minutes more entered Blowsabel again, holding in her hand a psalm-book with some words of an inscription on it in the handwriting of the elder, but subscribed "a friend," whereas, as the reader may recollect, the inscription in the book given to the first Helen, (with the misnomer of Janet,) was in the name of Andrew Gebbie—a fact rather in favour of Nelly *secunda*, insomuch as it harmonised

I

with her statement that the friendship between the elder and her had been kept a secret known only to themselves.

"That goes for what it's worth," said she, as she received back the book. "And now," she continued, addressing Mr Crawford, "you can tell me whether you were able to find, within the hail o' Edinburgh, a single person who knew that Elder Andrew had six taes on his left foot."

"I have found no one," was the answer, "for the good reason that Andrew Gebbie had no more toes on his left foot than you yourself have on yours."

Whereupon Helen *secunda* burst out into a laugh. After which, said she, "I will prove it, as sure as I am a living woman!"

"The man is dead and buried!" replied Mr Crawford, with a voice of triumph.

"That makes nae difference," said she; "unless it be that the worms have eaten awa the sixth tae; and, by my faith, I'll see to it!"

And with these words she went away, leaving the trustees in as great a difficulty as ever. Nor had she been long gone when a man of the name of Marshall, the procurator who had taken up the case of the first Helen, entered and said, "he had got evidence to show that a neighbour, who had been present at the last interview between the elder and his client, had heard the worthy man declare, that he had been moved to pity by her age and poverty, and had promised to do something for her, to enable her to pass her remaining years in comfort."

"But," said the agent, "there is, I am sorry to say, another Helen in the field; and you must drive her off before we can pay your client the money."

"And I know who she is," was the answer. "That woman's word is not to be relied upon; for she is what she is." And then he added, "I am determined to see justice done to my client—who, at least, is an honest woman."

"Now you see, gentlemen," said Mr Crawford, after the first Helen's agent had departed—"you see how this extraordinary affair stands. The two claimants are determined to fight it out: so that, if you pay the money to the good woman, you will, as I said before, run a risk of being obliged to pay the other one afterwards out of your stipends."

"Our stipends are the holy tenths, set apart to the work of the Lord from the beginning of the world," answered the brethren, "and cannot be touched, except by sacrilegious hands!"

"Then," continued the agent, "there is only one thing we can do; and that is, to throw the case into court by what we call a multiplepoinding, and let the claimants fight against each other."

A proposition this to which the trustees felt themselves bound to agree, though with very much reluctance; for they saw that the case would become public, and there would be ill-disposed people that would be inclined to put a false construction upon the motives of the worthy elder of Trinity. But then, to comfort them, they felt assured that the story of the toes was a pure invention; and the elder being buried, there was no possibility of proving the same.

Whereupon the meeting separated. Next day Mr Crawford commenced his law proceedings; and in due time, a record having been prepared, the advocates behoved to plead the causes of their respective clients.

Then stood up Mr Anderson, the advocate of the first Helen, and said :—

"Your lordships must see that—if you lay out of view as a mere invention, which it is, the story of the six toes—the preponderance of the evidence lies with my client. There is a psalm-book in each case; but mine has the name of the testator to the inscription: and you have, in addition, the testimony of one respectable person who heard Mr Gebbie declare his intention to enable this poor old woman to live. On the other side you have no evidence whatever that the elder ever set his foot—corns or no corns—on the floor of the Helen *secunda*. There was no such *footing* of intimacy as that contended for on the other side ; and that I am justified in calling the story of the six toes an invention will appear when I say that, according to the authority of learned men, a *lusus naturæ* of this kind does not occur once in ten thousand births : so that it is ten thousand to one against the assumption. In addition, there is the character of the deceased, whose whole life and conversation are against the presumption that he would go to Leith Wynd, and get a woman of doubtful character to operate upon a foot of which he is said to have been ashamed. For all which reasons I claim the three hundred pounds for my client."

Then stood up Mr Sharp, the advocate of the second Helen, and said :—

"It is no wonder at all why my learned friend has a difficulty about his *locus standi*, seeing he is so delicate about the feet. I feel no delicacy on that fundamental point. And it is because my corns of legal right and justice are pared that I stand here with so much ease, and assert that Mr Gebbie having imparted to my client a secret which he never communicated to living mortal besides, that secret could only have been the result of an intimacy and confidence sufficient to justify this legacy in her favour of three hundred pounds. My friend says, that there are many chances against such a freak of nature as six toes. That is true. But he confounds the thing with the assertion of the thing. And were there not a presumption in favour of a person speaking the truth rather than falsehood, what would become of that testimony which is the foundation of our holy religion, not less than of the decisions of our courts of justice? But it is in the power of this court to ascertain the truth of my assertion. The body of the worthy elder can be exhumed; and if it shall appear that it has six toes on the left foot, the presumption of the intimacy of friendship which will justify the legacy is complete. On the other side there is no such presumption. The elder only visited the first Helen once or twice, and what was to induce him to leave her so large a sum to the deprivation of his poor relations?"

Then the President spoke as follows:—

"It appears to the Court that, in this very extraordinary case, we never can get at the truth without testing, by proof, the statement made by the second Helen in regard to the six toes, because if it is really a fact that the testator carried this number on his left foot, and by parity that that number carried him, it is impossible to get quit of the presumption that the fact was communicated confidentially when the operation of paring was resorted to; and as confidence implies friendship, and friendship intimacy, we must assume that there must have been such an amount of mutual liking on the part of these individuals as would justify the legacy which is the subject-matter of this multipleoinding. The Court will therefore issue an order for the exhumation of the body of Andrew Gebbie, for the purpose of ascertaining whether the testator's foot was formed in the manner asserted by the claimant."

The commission was accordingly issued. The body of the elder was examined as it lay in the coffin, and the result of the examination, as stated in the report, was: "That the left foot was furnished with six toes, the sixth or supernumerary one being much smaller than the one next to it. It also appeared that the toes of this foot were supplied with a number of very hard corns, which bore the marks of having been often pared by some very careful hand."

Whereupon the case was again taken up, when judgment was given for the second Helen, who was thus remarkably well paid for her attention to the corns of the worthy elder. When the decision was reported to the reverend executors, Father

Tron shook his head with great gravity, Tolbooth did the same, and so did Trinity: nay, they all shook their heads at the same time: but what they intended to signify thereby was never known, for the reason that it was never declared.

## The Story of Mysie Craig.

IN detailing the curious circumstances of the following story, I am again only reporting a real law case to be found in the Court of Session Records, the turning-point of which was as invisible to the judges as to the parties themselves—that is, until the end came; a circumstance again which made the case a kind of developed romance. But as an end implies a beginning, and the one is certainly as necessary as the other, we request you to accompany us—taking care of your feet—up the narrow spiral staircase of a tenement called Corbet's Land, in the same old town where so many wonderful things in the complicated drama—or dream, if you are a Marphurius—of human life have occurred. Up which spiral stair having got by the help of our hands, almost as indispensable as that of the feet—we find ourselves in a little human dovecot of two small rooms, occupied by two persons not unlike, in many respects, two doves

—Widow Craig and her daughter, called May, euphuised by the Scotch into Mysie. The chief respects in which they might be likened, without much stress, to the harmless creatures we have mentioned, were their love for each other, together with their total inoffensiveness as regarded the outside world; and we are delighted to say this, for we see so many of the multitudinous sides of human nature dark and depraved, that we are apt to think there is no bright side at all. Nor shall we let slip the opportunity of saying, at the risk of being considered very simple, that of all the gifts of felicity bestowed, as the Pagan Homer tells, upon mankind by the gods, no one is so perfect and beautiful as the love that exists between a good mother and a good daughter.

For so much we may be safe by having recourse to instinct, which is deeper than any secondary causes we poor mortals can see. But beyond this, there were special reasons tending to this same result of mutual affection, which come more within the scope of our observation. In explanation of which we may say that the mother, having something in her power during her husband's life, had foreseen the advantages of using it in the instruction of her quick and intelligent daughter in an art of far more importance then than now—that of artistic needlework. Nay, of so much importance was this beautiful art, and to such perfection was it brought at a time when a lady's petticoat, embroidered by the hand, with its profuse imitations of natural objects, flowers, and birds, and strange devices, would often cost twenty pounds Scots, that a sight of one of those operose achievements of genius would make us blush for our time and the labours of our women. Nor was the perfection in this ornamental industry a new thing, for the daughters of the Pictish kings confined in the castle were adepts in it; neither was it left altogether to paid sempstresses, for great ladies spent their time in it, and emulation quickened both the genius and the diligence. So we need hardly say it became to the mother a thing to be proud of, that her daughter Mysie proved herself so apt a scholar that she became an adept, and was soon known as one of the finest embroideresses in the great city. So, too, as a consequence, it came to pass that great ladies employed her, and often the narrow spiral staircase of Corbet's Land was brushed on either side by the huge masses of quilted and emblazoned silk that, enveloping the belles of the day, were with difficulty forced up to, and down from, the small room of the industrious Mysie.

But we are now speaking of art, while we should have more to say (for it concerns us more) of the character of the young woman who was destined to figure in a stranger way than in making beautiful figures on silk. Mysie was one of a class; few in number they are indeed, but on that account more to be prized. Her taste and fine manipulations were but counterparts of qualities of the heart—an organ to which the pale face, with its delicate lines, and the clear liquid eyes, was a suitable index. The refinement which enabled her to make her imitation of beautiful objects on the delicate material of her work was only another form of a sensibility which pervaded her whole nature—that gift which is only conceded to peculiar organisations, and is such a doubtful one, too, if we go, as we cannot help doing, with the poet, when he sings that "chords that vibrate sweetest pleasures," often also "thrill the deepest notes of woe." Nay, we might say that the creatures themselves seem to fear the gift, for they shrink from the touch of the rough world, and retire within themselves as if to avoid it, while they are only courting its effects in the play of an imagination much too ardent for the duties of life. And, as a consequence, how they seek secretly the support of stronger natures, clinging to them as do those strange plants called parasites, which, with their tender arms and something so like fingers, cling to the nearest stem of a stouter neighbour, and embracing it, even though hollow and rotten, cover it, and choke it with a flood of flowers. So true is it that woman, like the generous vine, lives by being supported and held up; yet equally true that the strength she gains is from the embrace she gives, and so it is also that goodness, as our Scottish poet Home says, often wounds itself, and affection proves the spring of sorrow.

All which might truly be applied to Mysie Craig; but as yet the stronger stem to which she clung was her mother, and it was not likely, nor was it in reality, that that affection would prove to her anything but the spring of happiness, for it was ripened by love, and the earnings of the nimble fingers, moving often into the still hours of the night, not only kept the wolf from the door, but let in the lambs of domestic harmony and peace. Would that these things had so continued; but there are other wolves than those of poverty, and the "ae lamb o' the fauld" cannot be always under the protection of the ewe; and so it happened on a certain night, not particularised in the calendar, that our Mysie, having finished one of these floral petticoats on which she had been engaged for many weeks, went forth with her precious burden to deliver the same to its impatient owner—no other than the then famous Anabella Gilroy, who resided in Advocate's Close. Of which fine lady, by the way, we may say that of all the gay creatures who paraded between "the twa Bows," no one displayed such ample folds of brocaded silk, nodded her pon-pons more jantily, or napped with a sharper crack her high-heeled shoes, all to approve herself to "the bucks" of the time, with their square coats brocaded with lace, their three-cornered hats on the top of their bob-wigs, their knee-buckles and shoe-buckles. And certainly not the least important of those, both in his own estimation and that of the sprightly Anabella, was George Balgarnie, a young man who had only a year before succeeded to the property of Balgruddery, somewhere in the north, and of whom we might say that in forming him Nature had taken so much pains with the building up of the body, that she had forgotten the mind, so that he had no more spiritual matter in him than sufficed to keep his blood hot, and enable his sensual organs to work out their own selfish gratifications; or, to perpetrate a metaphor, he was all the polished mahogany of a piano, without any more musical springs than might respond to one keynote of selfishness. And surely Anabella had approved herself to the fop to some purpose, for when our sempstress with her bundle had got into the parlour of the fine lady, she encountered no other than Balgarnie—a circumstance apparently of very small importance, but we know that a moment of time is sometimes like a small seed, which contains the nucleus of a great tree, perhaps a poisonous one. And so it turned out that while Anabella was gloating over the beautiful work of the timid embroideress, Balgarnie was busy admiring the artist, but not merely, perhaps not at all, as an artist—only as an object over whom he wished to exercise power.

This circumstance was not unobserved by the little embroideress, but it was only observed to be shrunk from in her own timid way, and probably it would soon have passed from her mind, if it had not been followed up by something more direct and dangerous. And it was; for no sooner had Mysie got to the foot of the stairs than she encountered Balgarnie, who had gone out before her; and now began one of those romances in daily life of which the world is full, and of which the world is sick. Balgarnie, in short, commenced that kind of suit which is nearly as old as the serpent, and, therefore, not to be wondered at; neither are we to wonder that Mysie listened to it, because we have heard so much about "lovely woman stooping to folly," that we are content to put it to the large account of natural miracles. And not very miraculous either, when we remember, that if the low-breathed accents of tenderness awaken the germ of love, they awaken at the same time faith and trust; and such was the beginning of the romance which was to go through the normal stages—the appointment to meet again—the meeting itself—the others that followed—the extension of the moonlight walks, sometimes to the Hunter's Bog between Arthur's Seat and Salisbury Crags, and sometimes to the song-famed "Wells o' Weary." All which were just as sun and shower to the germ of the plant: the love grew and grew, and the faith grew and grew also which saw in him that which it felt in itself. Nay, if any of those moonlight-loving elves that have left their foot-marks in the fairy rings to be seen near St Anthony's Well had whispered in Mysie's ear, "Balgarnie will never make you his wife," she would have believed the words as readily as if they had impugned the sincerity of her own heart. In short, we have again the analogue of the parasitic plant: the very fragility and timidity of Mysie were at once the cause and consequence of her confidence. She would cling to him and cover him with the blossoms of her affection; nay, if there were unsoundness in the stem, these very blossoms would cover the rottenness.

This change in the life of the little sempstress could not fail to produce some corresponding change at home. We read smoothly the play we have acted ourselves—and so the mother read love in the daughter's eyes, and heard it, too, in her long sighs; nor did she fail to read the sign that the song which used to lighten her beautiful work was no longer heard; for love to creatures so formed as Mysie Craig is too serious an affair for poetical warbling. But she said nothing—for while she had faith in the good sense and virtue of her daughter, she knew also that there was forbearance due to one who was her support. Nor, as yet, had she reason to fear, for Mysie still plied her needle, and the roses and the lilies sprang up in all their varied colours out of the ground of the silk or satin as quickly and as beautifully as they were wont, though the lilies of her cheeks waxed paler as the days flitted. And why the latter should have been we must leave to the reader; for ourselves only hazarding the supposition that, perhaps, she already thought that Balgarnie should be setting about to make her his wife—an issue which behoved to be the result of their intimacy sooner or later, for that in her simple mind there should be any other issue was just about as impossible as that, in the event of the world lasting as long, the next moon would not, at her proper time, again shine in that green hollow, between the Lion's Head and Samson's Ribs, which had so often been the scene of their happiness. Nay, we might say that though a doubt on the subject had by any means got into her mind, it would not have remained there longer than it took a shudder to scare the wild thing away.

Of course, all this was only a question of time; but certain it is that by and by the mother could see some connexion between Mysie's being more seldom out on those moonlight nights than formerly, and a greater paleness in her thin face, as if the one had been the cause of the other; but still she said nothing, for she daily expected that Mysie would herself break the subject to her, and so she was left only to increasing fears that her daughter's heart and affections had been tampered with, and perhaps she had fears that went farther. Still, so far as yet had gone, there was no remission in the labours of Mysie's fingers, as if in the midst of all—whatever that all might be—she recognised the paramount necessity of bringing in by those fingers the required and usual amount of the means of their livelihood. Nay, somehow or other, there was at that very time when her cheek was at the palest, and her sighs were at their longest, and her disinclination to speak was at the strongest, that the work increased upon her; for was not there a grand tunic to embroider for Miss Anabella, which was wanted on a given day—and were there not other things for Miss Anabella's friend, Miss Allardice, which were not to be delayed beyond that same day. And so she stitched and stitched on and on, till sometimes the little lamp seemed to go out for want of oil, while the true cause of her diminished light was really the intrusion of the morning sun, against which it had no chance. It might be, too, that her very anxiety to get these grand dresses finished helped to keep out of her mind ideas which could have done her small good, even if they had got in.

But at length the eventful hour came when the gentle sempstress withdrew the shining needle, made clear by long use, from the last touch of the last rose; and, doubtless, if Mysie had not been under the cloud of sorrow we have mentioned, she would have been happier at the termination of so long a labour..than she had ever been, for the finishing evening had always been a great occasion to both the inmates; nay, it had been always celebrated by a glass of strong Edinburgh ale— a drink which, as both a liquor and a liqueur, was as famous then as it is at this day. But of what avail was this work-termination to her now? Was it not certain that she had not seen Balgarnie for two moons, and though the impossibility of his not marrying her was just as impossible as ever, why were these two moons left to shine in the green hollow and on the rising hill without the privilege of throwing the shadows of Mysie Craig and George Balgarnie on the grass, where the fairies had left the traces of their dances? Questions these which she was unable to answer, if it were not even that she was afraid to put them to herself. Then, when was it that she felt herself unable to tie up her work in order to take it home, and that her mother, seeing the reacting effect of the prior sleepless nights in her languid frame, did this little duty for her, even as while she was doing it she looked through her tears at her changed daughter? But Mysie would do so much. While the mother should go to Miss Allardice, Mysie would proceed to Miss Anabella—and so it was arranged. They went forth together, parting at the Netherbow; and Mysie, in spite of a weakness which threatened to bring her with her burden to the ground, struggled on to her destination. At the top of Advocate's Close she saw a man hurry out and increase his step even as her eye rested on him; and if it had not appeared to her to be among the ultimate impossibilities of things, natural as well as unnatural, she would have sworn that that man was George Balgarnie; but then, it just so happened that Mysie came to the conclusion that such a circumstance was among these ultimate impossibilities.

This resolution was an effort which cost her more than the conviction would have done, though doubtless she did not feel this at the time, and so with a kind of forced step she mounted the stair, but when she got into the presence of Miss Gilroy she could scarcely pronounce the words—

"I have brought you the dress, ma'am."

"And I am so delighted, Miss Craig, that I could almost take you into my arms," said the lady; "but what ails ye, dear? You are as white as any snow I ever saw, whereas you ought to have been as blithe as a bridesmaid, for don't you know that you have brought me home one of my marriage dresses? Come now, smile when I tell you that to-morrow is my wedding-day."

"Wedding-day," muttered Mysie, as she thought of the aforesaid utter impossibility of herself not being soon married to George Balgarnie, an impossibility not rendered less impossible by the resolution she had formed not to believe that within five minutes he had flown away from her.

"Yes, Miss Craig, and surely you must have heard who the gentleman is, for does not the town ring of it from the castle to the palace, from Kirk-o'-Field to the Calton?"

"I have not been out," said Mysie.

"That accounts for it," continued the lady; "and I am delighted at the reason, for wouldn't it have been terrible to think that my marriage with George Balgarnie of Balgruddery was a thing of so small a note as not to be known everywhere?"

If Mysie Craig had appeared shortly before to Miss Gilroy paler than any snow her ladyship had ever seen, she must now have been as pale as some other kind of snow that nobody ever saw. The dreadful words had, indeed, produced the adequate effect—but not in the most common way, for we are to keep in view that it is not the most shrinking and sensitive natures that are always the readiest to faint; and there was, besides, the aforesaid conviction of impossibility which, grasping the mind by a certain force, deadened the ear to words implying the contrary. Mysie stood fixed to the spot, as if she were trying to realise some certainty she dared not think was possible, her lips apart, her eyes riveted on the face of the lady —mute as that kind of picture which a certain ancient calls a silent poem, and motionless as a figure of marble.

An attitude and appearance still more inexplicable to Anabella, perhaps irritating as an unlucky omen, and, therefore, not possessing any claim for sympathy—at least, it got none.

"Are you the Mysie Craig," she cried, as she looked at the girl, "who used to chat to me about the dresses you brought, and the flowers on them? Ah, jealous and envious, is that it? But, you forget, George Balgarnie never could have made *you* his wife—a working needlewoman; he only fancied you as the plaything of an hour. He told me so himself when I charged him with having been seen in your company. So, Mysie, you may as well look cheerful. Your turn will come next, with some one in your own station."

There are words which stimulate and confirm—there are others that seem to kill the nerve and take away the sense, nor can we ever tell the effect till we see it produced; and so we could not have told beforehand—nay, we would have looked for something quite opposite—that Mysie, shrinking and irritable as she was by nature, was saved from a faint, (which had for some moments been threatening her,) by the cruel insult which thus had been added to her misfortune. She had even power to have recourse to that strange device of some natures, that of "affecting to be not affected;" and, casting a glance at the fine lady, she turned and went away without uttering a single word. But who knows the pain of the conventional concealment of pain, except those who have experienced the agony of the trial? Even at the moment when she heard that George Balgarnie was to be married, and that she came to know that she had been for weeks sewing the marriage dress of his bride, she was carrying under her heart the living burden which was the fruit of her love for that man. Yet not the burden of shame and dishonour, as our story will show, for she was justified by the law of her country—yea, by certain words once written by an apostle to the Corinthians, all which may as yet appear a great mystery; but, as regards Mysie Craig's agony, as she staggered down Miss Gilroy's stairs on her way home, there could be no doubt or mystery whatever.

Nor, when she got home, was there any comfort there for the daughter who had been so undutiful as to depart from her mother's precepts, and conceal from her not only her unfortunate connexion with a villain, but the condition into which that connexion had brought her. But she was, at least, saved from the pain of a part of the confession, for her mother had learned enough from Miss Allardice to satisfy her as to the cause of her daughter's change from the happy creature she once was, singing in the long nights as she wrought unremittingly at her beautiful work, and the poor, sighing, pale, heart-broken thing she had been for months. Nor did she fail to see, with the quick eye of a mother, that as Mysie immediately on entering the house laid herself quietly on the bed, and sobbed in her great agony, that she had learned the terrible truth from Miss Gilroy that the robe she had embroidered was to deck the bride of her destroyer. Moreover, her discretion enabled her to perceive that this was not the time for explanation, for the hours of grief are sacred, and the heart must be left to do its work by opening the issues of Nature's assuagement, or ceasing to beat. So the night passed, without question or answer; and the following day, that of the marriage, was one of silence, even as if death had touched the tongue that used to be the medium of cheerful words and tender sympathies—a strange contrast to the joy, if not revelry, in Advocate's Close.

It was not till after several days had passed that Mysie was able, as she still lay in bed, to whisper, amidst the recurring sobs, in the ear of her mother, as the latter bent over her, the real circumstances of her condition; and still, amidst the trembling words, came the vindication that she considered herself to be as much the wife of George Balgarnie as if they had been joined by " Holy Kirk;" a statement which the mother could not understand, if it was not to her a mystery, rendered even more mysterious by a reference which Mysie made to the law of the country, as she had heard the same from her cousin George Davidson, a writer's clerk in the Lawnmarket. Much of which, as it came in broken syllables from the lips of the disconsolate daughter, the mother put to the account of the fond dreams of a mind put out of joint by the worst form of misery incident to young women.

But what availed explanations, mysteries or no mysteries, where the fact was patent that Mysie Craig lay there, the poor heart-broken victim of man's perfidy—her powers of industry broken and useless—the fine weaving genius of her fancy, whereby she wrought her embroidered devices to deck and adorn beauty, only engaged now on portraying all the evils of her future life; and, above all, was she not soon to become a mother?

Meanwhile, and in the midst of all this misery, the laid-up earnings of Mysie's industry wore away, where there was no work by those cunning fingers —now thin and emaciated; and before the days passed, and the critical day came whereon another burden would be imposed on the household, there was need for the sympathy of neighbours in that form which soon wears out—pecuniary help. That critical day at length came. Mysie Craig gave birth to a boy, and their necessities from that hour grew in quicker and greater proportion than the generosity of friends. There behoved something to be done, and that without delay. So when Mysie lay asleep, with the innocent evidence of her misfortune by her side, Mrs Craig put on her red plaid and went forth on a mother's duty, and was soon in the presence of George Balgarnie and his young wife. She was under an impulse which made light of delicate conventionalities, and did not think it necessary to give the lady an opportunity of being absent; nay, she rather would have her to be present—for was she, who had been so far privy to the intercourse between her husband and Mysie, to be exempt from the consequences which she, in a sense, might have been said to have brought about?

"Ye have ruined Mysie Craig, sir!" cried at once the roused mother. "Ye have ta'en awa her honour. Ye have ta'en awa her health. Ye have ta'en awa her bread. Ay, and ye have reduced three human creatures to want, it may be starvation; and I have come here in sair sorrow and necessity to ask when and whaur is to be the remeid?"

"When and where you may find it, woman!" said the lady, as she cast a side-glance to her husband, probably by way of appeal for the truth of what she thought it right to say. "Mr Balgarnie never injured your daughter. Let him who did the deed yield the remeid!"

"And do you stand by this?" said Mrs Craig.

But the husband had been already claimed as free from blame by his wife, who kept her eye fixed upon him; and the obligation to conscience, said by sceptics to be an offspring of society, is sometimes weaker than what is due to a wife, in the estimation of whom a man may wish to stand in a certain degree of elevation.

"You must seek another father to the child of your daughter," said he, lightly. And, not content with the denial, he supplemented it by a laugh, as he added, "When birds go to the greenwood, they must take the chance of meeting the goshawk."

"And that is your answer?" said she.

"It is; and you need never trouble either my wife or me more on this subject," was the reply.

"Then may the vengeance o' the God of justice light on the heads o' baith o' ye!" added Mrs Craig, as she went hurriedly away.

Nor was her threat intended as an empty one, for she held on her way direct to the Lawnmarket, where she found George Davidson, to whom she related as much as she had been able to get out of Mysie, and also what had passed at the interview with Balgarnie and his lady. After hearing which, the young writer shook his head.

"You will get a trifle of aliment," said he; "perhaps half-a-crown a week, but no more; and Mysie could have made that in a day by her beautiful work."

"And she will never work mair," said the mother, with a sigh.

"For a hundred years," rejoined he, more to himself than to her, and probably in congratulation of himself for his perspicacity, "and since ever there was a college of justice, there never was a case where a man pulled up on oath for a promise of marriage admitted the fact. It is a good Scotch law—only we want a people to obey it. But what," he added again, "if we were to try it, though it were only as a grim joke and a revenge in so sad and terrible a case as that of poor Mysie Craig!"

Words which the mother understood no more than she did law Latin; and so she was sent away as sorrowful as she had come, for Davidson did not want to raise hopes which there was no chance of being fulfilled; but he knew as a Scotchman that a man who trusts himself to "a strae rape" in the hope of its breaking, may possibly hang himself, and so it happened that the very next day a summons was served upon George Balgarnie, to have it found and declared by the Lords of Session that he had promised to marry Mysie Craig, whereupon a child had been born by her; or, in fault of that, he was bound to sustain the said child. Thereupon, without the ordinary law's delay, certain proceedings went on, in the course of which Mysie herself was examined as the mother to afford what the lawyers call a *semiplena probatio*, or half proof, to be supplemented otherwise, and thereafter George Balgarnie stood before the august fifteen. He denied stoutly all intercourse with

Mysie, except an occasional walk in the Hunter's Bog; and this he would have denied also, but he knew that he had been seen, and that it would be sworn to by others; and then came the last question, which Mr Greerson, Mysie's advocate, put in utter hopelessness. Nay, so futile did it seem to try to catch a Scotchman by advising him to put his head in a noose on the pretence of seeing how it fitted his neck, that he smiled even as the words came out of his mouth—

"Did you ever promise to marry Mysie Craig?"

Was prudence, the chief of the four cardinal virtues, ever yet consistent with vice? Balgarnie waxed clever—a dangerous trick in a witness. He stroked his beard with a smile on his face, and answered—

"*Yes, once—when I was drunk!*"

Words which were immediately followed by the crack of a single word in the dry mouth of one of the advocates—the word "NICKED."

And nicked he was; for the presiding judge, addressing the witness, said—

"The drunkenness may be good enough in its own way, sir; but it does not take away the effect of your promise—nay, it is even an aggravation, insomuch as having enjoyed the drink, you wanted to enjoy with impunity what you could make of the promise also."

If Balgarnie had been a reader he might have remembered Waller's verse—

> "That eagle's fate and mine are one,
> Which on the shaft that made him die
> Espied a feather of his own,
> Wherewith he wont to soar so high."

So Mysie gained her plea, and the marriage with Anabella, for whom she had embroidered the marriage gown, was dissolved. How matters progressed afterwards for a time we know not; but the Scotch know that there is wisdom in making the best of a bad bargain, and in this case it was a good one; for, as the Lady of Balgruddery, Mysie Craig did no dishonour to George Balgarnie, who, moreover, found her a faithful wife, and a good mother to the children that came of this strange marriage.

## The Story of Pinched Tom.

IN searching again Lord Kilkerran's Session Papers in the Advocates' Library, I observed a strange remark written on the margin of one of them—"Beware of pinched Tom"—the meaning of which I was at a loss to find. His lordship was known to be a very grave man, as well as an excellent lawyer, and all so unlike the Newtons and Harmands, who made the blind Lady Justice laugh by the antics of that other lady sung by Béranger—Dame Folly—that I was put to my wit's end, although I admit that, by a reference to a part of the printed Session Papers opposite to which the remark was made, I thought I could catch a glimmering of his lordship's intention. The law case occupying the papers comprehended a question of disputed succession, and that question involved the application of a curious law in Scotland, which still remains. I believe we borrowed it from that great repertory from which our forefathers took so much wisdom

—the Roman code; but be that as it may, (and it's no great matter in so far as regards my story,) certain it is that it is a part of our jurisprudence, that where a marriage is dissolved by the death of the wife within a year and a day of the celebration thereof, without leaving a living child, the tocher goes back to the wife's friends. Of course nothing is more untrue than that bit of connubial wit: that while we hold, according to the Bible, that a man and his wife are *one*, we also very sensibly hold that the husband is *that one*. Then the child behoves to be a living child; but what constituted a living child often turned out to be as difficult a question as what constitutes a new birth of a living Christian, according to our good old sturdy Calvinism; for as all doctors know that a child will, on coming into the world, give a breath or two with a shiver, and then go off like a candle not properly lighted, it became a question whether, in such a case, the child could be said to have lived. Sometimes, too, the living symptom is less doubtful, as in the case, also very common, where the little stranger gives a tiny scream, the consequence of the filling of the lungs by the rushing in of the air, and having experienced a touch of the evils of life, makes up its mind to be off as quickly as possible from a wicked world. Now this last symptom our Scotch law accepts as the only evidence which can be received that the child had within it a living spirit, or, as we call it, an immortal soul. It would be of no importance that it opened and shut its eyes, moved its hands, or kicked or sprawled in any way you please; all this is nothing but infantine pantomime, and the worst pantomime, too, that it has no possible meaning that any rational person could understand, and so, therefore, it goes for nothing. In short, our law holds that, unless " baby squeak," there is no evidence that baby ever lived. Nor is any distinction made between the male and the female, although we know so well that the latter is much more inclined to make a noise than the other, were it for nothing else than to exhibit a first attempt to do that at which the sex are so good when they grow up and get husbands.

To bring back the reader to Lord Kilkerran's remark—" Beware of Pinched Tom "—the case to which the note applied comprehended the question whether the child had been heard to cry, and though the connexion might be merely imaginary on my part, I recollected in the instant having heard the story I now relate of Mr Thomas Whitelaw, a merchant burgess of Edinburgh, who figured somewhere between the middle and the end of last century, and took for wife a certain Janet Monypenny. In which union " the sufficient reason " which always exists, though we do not always know it, was on the part of the said Thomas the certainty that Janet's name (defying Shakespeare's question) was a real designative of a quality, that being that she possessed, in her own right, not merely many a penny, but so many thousand pennies, that they amounted to somewhere about two thousand merks, a large sum in those olden days. And this money was perhaps the more valuable, that the heiress had an unfortunate right by inheritance to consumption, whereby she ran a risk of being taken away, leaving her money unconsumed in the hands of her husband; an event, this latter, which our merchant burgess could certainly have turned to more certain account if he had provided against the law we have mentioned by entering into an antenuptial contract of marriage, wherein it might have been set forth that, though the marriage should be dissolved by the death of the wife before "year and day," without a living child being born thereof, yet the husband's right to the tocher would remain. But then Burgess Thomas did not know of any such law, while Mr George Monypenny, the brother of Mrs Janet, knew it perfectly, the more by token that he was a writer, that is, a legal practitioner, at the Luckenbooths. And though Mr George might have made a few pennies by writing out the contract, he never hinted to his intended brother-in-law of the propriety of any such act, because he knew that he had a chance of coming to more pennies, by the death of his sister, within the year and the day.

So the marriage was entered into without more use of written paper than what we call the marriage lines, and Writer George was satisfied until he began to see that Mrs Whitelaw was likely to be a mother before the expiry of the year and the day; but then he had the consolation—for, alas! human nature was the same in those olden times that it is now—of seeing that, while poor Janet was increasing in one way, she was decreasing in another, so that it was not unlikely that there would be not only a dead child, but a dead mother; and then he would come in as nearest of kin for the tocher of two thousand merks, of all which speculations on the part of the unnatural brother, Burgess Thomas knew nothing. But it so happened that Mrs Euphan Lythgow, the most skilly howdie or midwife in Edinburgh at that time, was the woman who was to bring the child into the world, and she had seen indications enough to satisfy her that there was a probability that things would go on in the very way so cruelly hoped for by the man of the law; nay, she had her eyes—open enough at all times—more opened still by some questions put to her by the wily expectant, and so she held it to be her duty to go straight to Burgess Thomas.

"I fear," said she, "baith for the mother and the bairn, for she is worn awa to skin and bane, and if she bear the heir she will only get lighter, as we ca' it, to tak on a heavier burden, even that o' death. The bairn may live, but it's only a chance."

Whereat Burgess Thomas looked sad, for he really loved his wife, but it might just happen that a thought came into his head that death had no power over the two thousand merks.

"If baith the mother and the bairn dee," continued Euphan, "the money you got by her will tak wing and flee awa to Mr George, her brother."

"What mean you, woman?" asked Mr Whitelaw, as he looked wistfully and fearfully into the face of the howdie.

"Had ye no' a contract o' marriage?" continued she.

"No," was the answer.

"Aweel, ye're in danger, for ken ye na it is our auld Scotch law that when there's nae contract, and the year and the day hasna passed, and when the mither dees and the bairn dees without a cry, the tocher flees back again? Heard ye never the auld rhyme—

> 'Mither dead and bairn gane,
> Pay the tocher to her kin;
> But an ye hear the bairn squeal,
> Gudeman, grip the tocher weel.'"

"God bless me, Mrs Lythgow! is that the law?" cried the husband, in a fright.

"Indeed, and it is," was the rejoinder. "You are muckle obliged to Writer George. If the bairn lives to be baptized, George is no the name it will bear."

"No," replied he; "if a boy, it will be baptized Thomas."

"Tam!" ejaculated the howdie in a screechy voice, the reason of which might be that her son carrying that name had died during the year, and she was affected.

But no sooner had the word Tam passed from her lips, than a large red cat came from the rug, and looking up in her face, mewed in so very expressive a way that the sadness which the recollection of her boy had inspired passed suddenly away, and was succeeded by a comical look; and rubbing Bawdrons "along of the hair," as Mr Dickens would express it, the true way of treating either cats or cat-witted people, she continued addressing the favourite—

"And you, Tam, and I will be better acquainted before the twa thousand merks are paid to Writer George."

"What does the woman mean?" said the burgess. "What connexion is there between that animal and my wife's fortune?"

"Ye'll ken that when the time comes," was the answer; "but coming nearer to the subject in hand, ye'll take care to hae twa witnesses in the blue-painted parlour, next to your bedroom, when I'm untwining the mistress o' her burden, whether it be a dead bairn or a living ane."

"And what good will that do me if both the mother and child should die?" inquired he.

"Ye'll ken that when Writer George comes and asks ye for the tocher," was the answer.

Nor did Mrs Euphan Lythgow wait to throw any further light upon a subject which appeared to the burgess to require more than the candle of his own mind could supply if he should snuff it again and again, and arn't we, every one of us, always snuffing the candle so often that we can see nothing? But Mrs Lythgow was what the Scotch people call "a skilly woman." She could see—to use an old and very common expression—as far into a millstone as any one, and it was especially clear to her that she would deliver Mrs Whitelaw of a dead child, that death would deliver the mother of her life, and Writer George would deliver Maister Whitelaw of two thousand good merks of Scotch money, unless, as a poor salvage out of all this loss, she could deliver the burgess out of the hands of the writer. And so the time passed till the eventful evening came, when the wasted invalid was seized with those premonitory pains which have come right down from old mother Eve to the fair daughters of men, as a consequence of her eating the too sweet paradise pippin. The indispensable Mrs Euphan Lythgow was sent for express and came on the instant, for she knew she had unusual duties to perform, nor did she forget as one of the chief of those to get Mrs Jean Gilchrist, a neighbouring gossip, and Robina Proudfoot, the servant, ensconsed in the said blue-painted parlour, for the sole end that they should hear what they could hear, but as for seeing anything that passed within the veil of the secret temple of Lucina, they were not to be permitted to get a glimpse until such time as might please the priestess of the mysteries herself.

All which secrecy has been followed by the unfortunate consequence that history nowhere records what took place in that secret room for an hour or two after the two women took up their station in the said blue-painted chamber. But this much we know, that the house was so silent that our favourite Tom could not have chosen a more auspicious evening for mousing for prey in place of mewing for play, even if he had had all the sagacity of the famous cats of Tartesia. As for Mrs Gilchrist and Robina, they could not have listened more zealously, we might even say effectually, if they had been gifted with ears as long as those of certain animals in Trophonia; and surely we cannot be wrong in saying they were successful listeners, when we are able to report that Mrs Gilchrist nipped the bare fleshy arm of Robina, as a sign that she heard what she wanted to hear.

"That's the scream o' the wean!" said she.

"Ay, and may the Lord be praised!" was the answer of Robina, in spite of the nip.

But neither the one nor the other knew that that cry was verily worth two thousand merks to Maister Burgess Whitelaw, the father, who in a back-room sat in the deep pit of anxiety and heard nothing, and perhaps it was better that he didn't, for that cry might have raised hopes—never to be realised—of the birth of a living son or daughter, who would by and by lisp in his ear the charmed word "Father"—of a dead wife's recovery, after so terrible a trial to one so much wasted—of the saving of his fortune from the ruthless hands of his brother-in-law. But there is always some consolation for the miserable, and didn't Mrs Janet's favourite, even Tom himself, with his bright scarlet collar, come to him and sit upon his knee and look up in his face and purr so audibly, that one might have thought he was expressing sympathy and hope? So it is: nature is always laughing at her own work. Even as this pantomine was acting, Mrs Lythgow opened the door of the blue-painted chamber, and presenting a bundle to Mrs Gilchrist—

"The bairn is dead," she whispered; "lay it on the table there out o' the sight o' its mother, who will not live lang enough even to see its dead face."

"And yet we heard it cry," said Robina. "Poor dear innocent," she added, as she peered among the folds of the flannel, "ye have had a short life."

"And no' a merry ane," added the gossip.

"Did ye expect the bairn to laugh, ye fule woman that ye are?" was the reply of the howdie. "Come and help me wi' the deeing mither."

And straightway the three women were by the bedside of the patient, in whose throat Death was already sounding his rattle, after the last effort of exhausted nature to give to the world a life in exchange for her own; and Mr Whitelaw was there too to witness the dying throes of his wife, with perhaps the thought in his mind that the gods are pitiless as well as foolish, for what was the use of giving him a dead child in recompense for a dead mother, and taking away from him, at the very same moment, the said two thousand merks of good Scotch money. Wherein, so far, Mr Whitelaw was himself unjust to these much abused gods; but he did not know as yet that the child had cried, and who knows what consoling effect that circumstance might have had upon one who was what Pindar calls "a man of money." At least, we will give to any man more than one of these merks who will show us out of the great "Treasury of Evils," mentioned by the Greek poets, any one which cannot be ameliorated by money. And so Mr Whitelaw heard, in the last expiring breath of Mrs Janet Monypenny the departing sign of the loss of the three greatest good things of this world—a wife, a child, and a tocher.

But the moral oscillation comes round as sure as that of the pendulum, and in accordance with that law Mr Whitelaw was, within a short time after the death of his wife, told by Mrs Gilchrist that the child had made the much-wished-for sign of life. A communication, this, very easily accounted for, but we do not undertake to explain why, when Mr Whitelaw heard it, he was scarcely equal to the task of preventing an expression upon his sorrowful countenance which an ill-natured person would call a smile. Nor, indeed, is there any way of explaining so inexplicable a phenomenon, except by having recourse to the fact mentioned by Burns, that "man is a riddle." A solution which will also serve us when we further narrate that this small wail of the child lightened wonderfully Mr Whitelaw's duty in getting all things arranged for the funeral, including the melancholy peculiarity of getting the coffin made that was to contain a mother and her first-born. Nay, it enabled him even at the funeral to meet the triumphant look of his brother-in-law, Writer George, as it clearly said, even in the midst of his tears, "You owe me two thousand merks;" for we are to remember that Mr Whitelaw, in exchange for the writer's perfidy in not mentioning to him the necessity of a contract of marriage, had with a spice of malice concealed from him the fact of the child having been heard to cry, and then it was natural for the writer to suppose that the child had been born dead.

As money ameliorates grief, business prevents grief from taking possession of the mind; and so we need not be surprised that within a week Mr Monypenny served Mr Whitelaw with a summons to appear before the fifteen Scotch lords who sat round a table in the form of a horse-shoe in the Parliament House of Edinburgh, or Court of Session, and there be ordered to pay to the pursuer or plaintiff the said two thousand merks, which devolved upon him, as the heir of his sister, in consequence of the dissolution of the marriage within a year and a day, without a living child being born thereof. Nor was Mr Whitelaw, angry as he was and withal confident of success, slow to give in his defence to the effect that the child had been born alive, and had been heard to scream—a defence which startled Writer George mightily; for it was the first intimation he had got of the important fact, and his experience told him how supple Scotch witnesses are—even to the extent that it took no fewer than fifteen learned judges to get the subtle thing called truth out of the subtle minds of "the canny people;" but he had no alternative than to consent to the commission to Maister Wylie, advocate, to take a proof of the defender's averment and report. And so accordingly the proceedings went on. Mr Advocate Wylie sat in one of the rooms adjoining the court to take the depositions of the witnesses, and Mr Williamson was there for Mr Whitelaw, and Mr Hamilton for Mr Monypenny. The first witness called was Mrs Jean Gilchrist, who swore very honestly that she heard the child scream; and Robina Proudfoot swore as honestly to the same thing; nor could all the efforts of Mr Advocate Hamilton shake those sturdy witnesses, if it was not that, as so often happens with Scotch witnesses, the more the advocate wrestled with them, the more firm they waxed. Nor need we say that the philosophical axiom, that the intensity of belief is always inversely as the reason for it, never had weight with our Scotch judges. But then came the difficulty about the *causa scientiæ*; for neither of the two witnesses could swear that she *saw* the child alive 'and after the scream, inasmuch as the child was certainly dead before they saw the body; so it was only at best a strong presumption that the cry actually did come from that child. The witnesses dispersed these quibbles, and insisted that, as there was no other child in that room, the cry could come from no other source than Mrs Whitelaw's baby. But the crowning witness was to come—Mrs Euphan Lythgow herself, who would put an end to all doubts; and come she did. Asked whether she delivered Mrs Whitelaw of a child on the night in question, her answer was in the affirmative.

"Was it a boy or a girl?"

"A *callant*, sir," was the answer; for Scotch witnesses *will* use their own terms, let counsel do what they please. "And," added Mrs Lythgow, "he was to be baptized after his father when the time came. He was to be called Tammas."

"Just so," continued Mr Hamilton; "and was he dead or alive when he was born?"

"Indeed, sir, little Tam was as life-like as you are when I handled him wi' thae hands."

"How do you know that?" was the next question.

"Ken whether a bairn is dead or living?" responded the midwife, with an ironical laugh. "Do dead bairns scream, think ye, Maister Hamilton? Ay, sir, I heard little Tam cry just as plainly as I hear you speak. It's God's way wi' mony a wean. They seem to ken it's an ill warld they're born into, wi' so mony lawyers in't, and they just gie a cry and gae awa back again."

And thus the evidence was concluded; nor did it ever occur to these hair-wigged and ear-wigged gentlemen to ask the astute howdie whether there was any other creature in the house (except Mr Thomas Whitelaw himself, who was out of the question) that bore the name of Tam; and Mrs Lythgow's conscience, like many others, sat as easy on the equivocation as a hen does on an addled egg with a shell like the rest, which contain little chickens all alive. And the case was virtually saved, as subsequently appeared, when the fifteen, all ear-wigged too, pronounced sentence in favour of the defender, Mr Whitelaw. But it was not till some time afterwards the real truth came out. "The labourer is worthy of his hire," and when Mrs Euphan called for fee, on Mr Whitelaw asking how much, the cunning howdie replied—

"Just a hundred merks, Maister Whitelaw."

"A hundred merks for bringing a child into the world, which lived no longer than to give a scream?"

"Ay, but you forget *pinched Tam*," replied she.

Whereupon Mr Whitelaw began to meditate, and thereupon ejaculated—"Oh! I see. Yes, yes; I did forget pinched Tam; and now I remember, he came into me that evening after you had ejected him from the bedroom."

"Surely, sir," rejoined the woman; "think ye I was fule enough to keep him in the room to be seen by the women, after I had got out o' him a' that I wanted?"

And Mrs Lythgow got her hundred merks. How the incident came to the ears of Lord Kilkerran, history saith not; but if you are curious, you may see upon the margin of the said Session Paper the words—"Beware of pinched Tom!"

## The Story of the Iron Press.

THE story of the Iron Press hung about my memory for years before I got it localised; nor do I know very well how it came to me, whether from the page of an old broad-sheet, or the tougher tongue of an old dame—the real vellum for the inscription of wonderful legends. However this may be, it is of small importance, inasmuch as I was subsequently so fortunate—and the word will be properly estimated by the real story-hunter—as to find myself in the very room where the recess of the press was still to be seen. How I did look at it, to be sure! nay, if it had been of gold—all my own, too—I question if I could have gazed into the dark recess with more interest; for gold, to people of my bias, is nothing in comparison with the enchantment that hangs about the real concrete *souvenir* of an old wonder. But before going further, I must apprise the English reader that the word "press"—a Scotch word of somewhat doubtful derivation (*maugre*

Jamieson)—is convertible into the more modern designation "cupboard," or rather "pantry;" with the qualification that our Scotch term more generally implies the adjunct of a door with lock and key.

With which help you may be induced to represent to yourself, as vividly as the fervour of your imagination may enable you, the house in Hyndford's Close, which, at the time wherein we are concerned, was occupied by a retired advocate called Mr George Plenderleith. You may see in it yet the signs of its old gentility. There are the panellings on the walls, the hooks whereon were suspended the flowered and figured draperies, the painted roofs, the peculiar enamelled sides of the chimneys having the appearance of china—all so very unlike our modern house fashions. It may not be that the iron press which was in the back bed-room, and the recess of which still remains, had anything to do with the fashion of the time; nor would it be easy to divine its use in a private gentleman's house, who had no ledgers, journals, or cash-books to preserve from fire, lest certain creditors might say they were burnt to help concealment. Perhaps it was for the conservation of some great property rights, or title-deeds as we call them; perhaps state papers—anything you like, but not the least unlikely, it may have been for the purpose of concealing some unfortunate Covenanter, who could still boast, in his pathetic way, that he had verily nowhere to lay his head; for the cell was too small for a reclining posture—nay, he could scarcely have got upon his knees to offer his Ebenezer for the preservation of the solemn league and covenant, and give thanks that he had got out of "the bishop's drag-net" and into an iron cage.

Most certainly, at least, this iron cage was not intended to immure the delicate person of the beautiful Ailsie Plenderleith, the only daughter of the advocate—nay, the greatest belle you could have met, displaying her gown of mazerine and her petticoat of cramosie, from "the castle on the knowe to the palace in the howe;" or, as the saying went, from "the castle gate to the palace yett." We don't doubt that our Miss Ailsie deserved all this high-flown praise; only we are to keep in mind that no young lady that ever figured in a legend, from the time of the Fair Maid of Troy to her of Perth, was ever anything less than an angel without wings. And in the case of our Ailsie, she might well have passed for possessing these appendages too, when we consider that she would not be behind her sister-belles in the size of those heavy folds of braided silk they drew through their pocket-holes, and seemed to fly with. We need not say that such a creature, if amiable in her mind and affections, would be doated on by such a father as Mr Plenderleith, who had now no wife to console him, and who would expect from his child at least as much love as he was willing to bestow on her. And so, to be sure, it was; he loved his dear Ailsie to what may be called paternal distraction, but as for how much dutiful affection Ailsie bestowed on him, we cannot say.

On another point we can be more sure, and that is, that although her father had many nice beaux in his eye who had a power to *dot*, and doubtless on so fine a subject no disinclination at all to *doat*, the never a one of them would the saucy Ailsie look upon except with that haughty disdain which, when it appears in a beautiful woman, is so apt to pique young admirers into greater adoration, mixed, it may be, sometimes with a little choler— a thing that is not so alien to love as you would imagine. Nor was the reason of all this cold *hauteur* any wonder at all when we are given to know that Miss Plenderleith had one day, by the merest chance, taken into her eye, and even to the back or innermost recesses thereof, the figure of a young student of " old Embro' College," called Frederick Lind, a poor bursar of no family, but blessed with what was ten thousand times of more importance in the estimation of the tasteful Ailsie—a handsome person, and a fine ruddy, intelligent face, which was lighted up with an eye as likely to drink up the form of Ailsie as hers had been to receive his. And no doubt it may appear very wonderful that Cupid, who is, as they say, as blind as a bat, and so hits by chance, should have the power of imparting to the eyes of his victims the faculty not only of seeing each other more clearly than before, but also of reading each other's eyes so plainly, that by a glance they know that they are mutually thinking of each other. But such, we all know very well, is the fact, and so Frederick Lind and Ailsie Plenderleith came to this state of knowledge, and not only so, they came to means of ascertaining, by actual conversation, whether such was really the case or not—the consequence of which was just the natural one, that the sympathy of this knowledge became the sympathy of love; and we suspect that if any one was to blame for this, it was Old Mother Nature herself, who is considerably stronger and more dogmatic in her opinions than either mother or father of earthly mould.

The connexion thus formed—we are compelled, though sorry, to say, clandestinely — might not have entailed upon the young devotees any very formidable consequences, had they been prudent, and confined their meetings to St Leonard's

Double-dykes, St Anthony's Well, the Giant's Ribs, the Hunter's Bog, or the Friar's Walk. Nay, they might have adventured even less recondite walks; but they had some notions of comfort which would be gratified with nothing short of a roof over their very irrational heads, and probably a fire burning by their sides, as if love could not have kept itself in fuel without the assistance of so coarse and earthy a thing as Midlothian coal.

While all this was going forward, and generating confidence in the ordinary ratio of successful immunity, our good and loving old Mr Advocate Plenderleith was just as busy with *his* eyes in endeavouring to find out among the said beaux of Edinburgh, with their braided broad-tailed coats and ruffled wristbands, of which Mr Frederick Lind had nothing to boast, such a one as would be likely to form a suitable husband to his pretty but scornful, (to all save one,) daughter, and a promising son-in-law to himself; that is, one who would bring a sum to the mutual exchequer, and take care not only of Ailsie, but that fine property of his in Lanarkshire, called Threemarks, from its valuation in the land-roll being of that very considerable extent. And so he did his best to invite one or two of them to his house in Hyndford's Close to drink a bottle of claret, and see Miss Ailsie through the charmed medium of the same, being satisfied that a young woman is seen to more advantage through that medium than through the roses of the Paphian groves where Venus dallies with her son. But all this paternal black-footing would not do, because the step went only in one direction, without a return. Our Ailsie scorned them all—a very unwise policy in the little rebel, for she might have seen that her father, who was a shrewd man, would be likely to suspect that the ship which rides at an anchor, however little seen, is just that very one which seems to defy most the blustering winds and the rolling waves. And accordingly Mr Plenderleith began to think that his daughter's heart must be anchored somewhere —not so likely on golden sands as on some tough clay—and *that* "where" he would have given his old Parliament-House wig, with all the meal in it to boot, to find out. Nay, he began to be angry before he could assure himself of the fact; and being as determined under a restrainer as he ever had been under a retainer, he was a dangerous man for even a loving daughter to tamper with.

But old fathers, probably with spectacles, are not good watchers of their love-stricken daughters; and Mr Plenderleith, knowing this, placed confidence in his old servant or servitor, (as these domestic Balderstones were then called,) Andrew Crabbin, and got him to keep an eye upon the outgoings and incomings, and companionship and letters of the unsuspecting Ailsie. On the other hand, she was inclined to place faith in Andrew—not that she let him know the name or degree of her beloved Frederick, but that she bespoke his secrecy in the event of his seeing her with a highly respectable young man, of genteel connexions, whom her father would be delighted to receive as a son-in-law, but who was not just yet in a position to present himself in the drawing-room. Which two confidences Andrew received together, and found means in his canny Scotch head to entertain both kindly, but with a foregone conclusion that he would make more money out of the rents and fees of his master than the pin-money of poor Ailsie.

Yet Miss Plenderleith was so dexterous in managing her intrigue, that Andrew had for a time nothing to reveal; but opportunity comes at the end to patience, and this was the case one night when Andrew was busy cleaning his master's long boots in an outhouse at the back of the dwelling-house; for as he was straining to get the article in his hand as bright as the "Day and Martin" of the time would make it, his attention was directed to a sound from the red-tiled roof. Whereupon, pricking up his ears, Andrew put his head out at the door, and what in all this wide earth does he see but two boots disappearing at Ailsie's bed-room window! He had never seen any of the two or three pairs his master possessed going into the house in that way, and probably he did not need that fact to explain to him the wonderful apparition. Nor was it any question with him what to do. The hour was late, but his master was not gone to bed, if he was not yet engaged over his mulled claret, with a bit of toast done pretty brown in it.

Having accordingly got, unobserved from above, into the back door—the more by reason that he waited till the window-sash came down with all prudential softness of sound—Andrew made his way up-stairs to the room where Mr Plenderleith was regaling himself, and probably thinking of the scornful Ailsie, who would not accord to his matrimonial wishes. "There's a young man gone in this minute at Miss Ailsie's bed-room window," said he, in a mysterious way, to his master; whereupon Mr Plenderleith started up in a great rage, and rushing to a closet brought forth a long rapier of formidable sharpness. "I will slay him on the spot," said he, "for it is hamesucken and a deuced deal more, and I have law on my side. Come with me, Andrew Crabbin." But Andrew's intermediate views did not accord with the slaughter of Ailsie's lover. "Wait," says he, "till I listen;" and hastening to Miss Plenderleith's room, he tirled at the door, so that it might be heard inside, but not by his enraged master, whose spirit was more in his fiery eye than his ear; and coming back more slowly than comported with his master's fury—"Now's your time," said he, "for I heard him inside." Nor was there now any time lost, for the infuriated father rushed along the lobby to his daughter's chamber door, which, to his surprise, he found unfastened; and, having entered, he found Ailsie all very much at her ease, nor was there anything to rouse his suspicions at all except the condition of the blind, which was drawn up. No more was needed—that was enough; the angry father accused his daughter with having had a man in her bed-room. Ailsie denied the charge, but it was of no avail. Orders were upon the instant issued to get the carriage ready, and in the course of an hour afterwards Mr Plenderleith and his daughter, with Andrew and the two female servants in a hired carriage, were on their way to his house at Threemarks. The house in Hyndford's Close was shut up. Mr Plenderleith had in so short a period made up his mind, and executed a purpose which he considered necessary to his own honour and his daughter's preservation.

Time passed on, and in the meantime Andrew

kept his secret, delighted in his own mind that he had saved the life of the young man. About a month afterwards Mr Plenderleith came to town alone, and having entered the house found everything precisely as he left it. But he had an object—no other than to discover whether Ailsie had left any letters whereby he might discover the name of the clandestine lover. So far he succeeded, and having returned to Threemarks, he some time afterwards despatched Andrew to Edinburgh to make inquiries as to a student of the name of Frederick Lind. This commission Andrew executed with fidelity, but all his efforts were vain; no tidings could be heard of the youth. The landlady with whom he had lodged said that he had gone out one night and had never returned; and the opinion of his relations, to whom she had communicated the fact of his absence, was, that he had gone to England, where he also had relations. With this account Mr Plenderleith was so far pleased, but he continued from time to time to repeat his inquiries with no better, or rather to him worse, success. Yet such was his apprehension lest his daughter should again have it in her power to deceive him, that he remained at Threemarks for the full space of three years and more.

Meanwhile Ailsie, having come to the conclusion that she would not see her lover again, renounced all thoughts of him except what perhaps at night would rise up to her fancy, when the internal lights play false with the reason. The young heart requires only time to renounce the strongest passion, though a cherished memory will still hang suspended over the sacred tomb of its affections. And so it was. More time passed, till at length Ailsie Plenderleith agreed to give her hand to a young advocate of the name of George Graham, who had good prospects at the bar. The couple were to be married in Hyndford's Close, and the house was put in order to receive them. Ailsie came in a bride. The ceremony was performed with great *éclat* and rejoicings. And now comes that part of the legend which always fits so well to some great occasion, such as a marriage; but we must take these things as we find them. The new-married couple were to sleep in the room which had been the scene of so strange a play three or four years ago. On returning to take off her bride's dress, her eye became fixed upon the door of the iron press. A wild thought seized her brain: she applied her finger to the well-known spring. The door opened, and the skeleton of Frederick Lind fell out against her, rattling in the clothes that hung about it, and striking her as it fell with a loud crash on the floor.

The explanation of our legend is not difficult.

Lind had been pushed into the press on previous occasions, without the door being closed entirely upon him. Ailsie, on the fatal evening, had no doubt thought that she had left the door as she used to do; but in the hurry consequent on the coming of her father, she had committed the terrible mistake of imparting to it too much impulse, whereby the lock had caught; and as the spring was not available inside, the prisoner was immured beyond the chance of escape. So narrow, too, was the recess, that the skeleton form had stood upright in the clothes, and it thus fell out when relieved of the support of the door.

## The Story of the Girl Forger.

IT is a common thing for writers of a certain class, when they want to produce the feeling of wonder in their readers, to introduce some frantic action, and then to account for it by letting out the secret that the actor was mad. The trick is not so necessary as it seems, for the strength of human passions is a potentiality only limited by experience; and so it is that a sane person may under certain stimulants do the maddest thing in the world. The passion itself is always true, it is only the motive that may be false; and therefore it is that in narrating for your amusement, perhaps I may add instruction, the following singular story—traces of the main parts of which I got in the old books of a former procurator-fiscal—I assume that there was no more insanity in the principal actor, Euphemia, or, as she was called, Effie, Carr, when she brought herself within the arms of the law, than there is in you, when now you are reading the story of her strange life. She was the only daughter of John Carr, a grain merchant, who lived in Bristo Street. It would be easy to ascribe to her all the ordinary and extraordinary charms that are thought so necessary to embellish heroines; but as we are not told what these were in her case, we must be contented with the assurance that nature had been kind enough to her to give her power over the hearts of men. We shall be nearer our purpose when we state, what is necessary to explain a peculiar part of our story, that her father, in consequence of his own insufficient education, had got her trained to help him in keeping his accounts with the farmers, and in writing up his books; nay, she enjoyed the privilege of writing his drafts upon the Bank of Scotland, which the father contrived to sign, though in his own illiterate way, and with a peculiarity which it would not have been easy to imitate.

But our gentle clerk did not consider these duties imposed upon her by her father as excluding her either from gratifying her love of domestic habits by assisting her mother in what at that time was denominated hussyskep or housekeeping, or from a certain other gratification, which might without a hint from us be anticipated—no other than the luxury of falling head and ears, and heart too we fancy, in love with a certain dashing young student of the name of Robert Stormonth, then attending the University more for the sake of polish than of mere study; for he was the son of the proprietor of Kelton, and required to follow no profession. How Effie got entangled with this youth we have no means of knowing, so we must be contented with the Scotch proverb—

> "Tell me where the flea may bite,
> And I will tell where love may light."

The probability is that, from the difference of their stations and the retiring nature of our gentle clerk, we shall be safe in assuming that he had, as the saying goes, been smitten by her charms in some of those street encounters, where there is more of Love's work done than in "black-footed" tea coteries expressly held for the accommodation of Cupid. And that the smitting was a genuine feeling we are not left to doubt, for, in addition to the reasons we shall afterwards have too good occasion to know, he treated Effie, not as those wild students who are great men's sons do "the light o' loves" they meet in their escapades; for he intrusted his secrets to her, he took such small counsel from her poor head as a "learned clerk" might be supposed able to give; nay, he told her of his mother, and how one day he hoped to be able to introduce her at Kelton as his wife. All which Effie repaid with the devotedness of that most wonderful affection called the first or virgin love—the purest, the deepest, the most thoroughgoing of all the emotions of the human heart. But as yet he had not conceded to her wish that he should consent to their love being made known to Effie's father and mother: love is only a leveller to itself and its object; the high-born youth, inured to refined manners, shrunk from a family intercourse, which put him too much in mind of the revolt he had made against the presumed wishes and intentions of his proud parents. Wherein, after all, he was only true to the instincts of that institution, apparently so inhumane as well as unchristian in its exclusiveness, called aristocracy; and yet with the excuse that its roots are pretty deeply set in human nature.

But, proud as he was, Bob Stormonth the younger, of Kelton, was amenable to the obligations of a necessity, forged by his own imprudent hands. He had, by a fast mode of living, got into debt—a condition from which his father, a stern man, had relieved him twice before, but with a threat on the last occasion that if he persevered in his prodigality he would withdraw from him his yearly allowance, and throw him upon his own resources. The threat proved ineffectual, and this young heir of entail, with all his pride, was once in the grasp of low-born creditors : nay, things in this evil direction had gone so far that writs were out against him, and one in the form of a caption was already in the hands of a messenger-at-arms. That the debts were comparatively small in amount was no amelioration where the purse was all but empty ; and he had exhausted the limited exchequers of his chums, which with college youths was, and is, not difficult to do. So the gay Bob was driven to his last shift, and that, as is generally the case, was a mean one ; for necessity, as the mother of inventions, does not think it proper to limit her births to genteel or noble devices to please her proud consort. He even had recourse to poor Effie to help him ; and, however ridiculous this may seem, there were reasons that made the application appear not so desperate as some of his other schemes. It was only the caption that as yet quickened his fears ; and as the sum for which the writ was issued was only twenty pounds, it was not, after all, so much beyond the power of a clerk.

It was during one of their ordinary walks in the Meadows that the pressing necessity was opened by Stormonth to the vexed and terrified girl. He told her that, but for the small help he required in the meantime, all would be ruined. The wrath of his father would be excited once more, and probably to the exclusion of all reconciliation; and he himself compelled to flee, but whither he knew not. He had his plan prepared, and proposed to Effie, who had no means of her own, *to take a loan* of the sum out of her father's cash-box—words very properly chosen according to the euphemistic policy of the devil, but Effie's genuine spirit was roused and alarmed.

"Dreadful!" she whispered, as if afraid that the night-wind would carry her words to honest ears. "Besides," she continued, "my father, who is a hard man, keeps his desk lockit."

Words which took Stormonth aback, for even he saw there was here a necessity as strong as his own; yet the power of invention went to work again.

"Listen, Effie," said he. "If you cannot help me, it is not likely we shall meet again. I am desperate, and will go into the army."

The ear of Effie was chained to a force which was direct upon the heart. She trembled and looked wistfully into his face, even as if by that look she could extract from him some other device less fearful by which she might have the power of retaining him for so short a period as a day.

"You draw out your father's drafts on the bank, Effie," he continued. "Write one out for me, and

I will put your father's name to it. You can draw the money. I will be saved from ruin; and your father will never know."

A proposal which again brought a shudder over the girl.

"Is it Robert Stormonth who asks me to do this thing?" she whispered again.

"No," said he; "for I am not myself. Yesterday, and before the messenger was after me, I would have shrunk from the suggestion. I am not myself, I say, Effie. Ay or no; keep me or lose me,—that is the alternative."

"Oh, I cannot," was the language of her innocence, and for which he was prepared; for the stimulant was again applied in the most powerful of all forms—the word farewell was sounded in her ear.

"Stop, Robert; let me think." But there was no thought, only the heart beating wildly. "I will do it; and may the penalty be mine, and mine only."

So it was: "even virtue's self turns vice when misapplied." What her mind shrank from was embraced by the heart as a kind of sacred duty of a love making a sacrifice for the object of its first worship. It was arranged; and as the firmness of a purpose is often in proportion to the prior disinclination, so Effie's determination to save her lover from ruin was forthwith put in execution; nay, there was even a touch of the heroine in her, so wonderfully does the heart, acting under its primary instincts, sanctify the device which favours its affection. That same evening Effie Carr wrote out the draft for twenty pounds on the Bank of Scotland, gave it to Stormonth, who from a signature of the father's, also furnished by her, perpetrated the forgery—a crime at that time punishable by death. The draft so signed was returned to Effie. Next forenoon she went to the bank, as she had often done for her father before; and the document being in her handwriting, as prior ones of the same kind had also been, no scrutinising eye was turned to the signature. The money was handed over, but *not counted* by the recipient, as before had been her careful habit—a circumstance with its effect to follow in due time. Meanwhile Stormonth was at a place of appointment out of the reach of the executor of the law, and was soon found out by Effie, who gave him the money with trembling hands. For this surely a kiss was due. We do not know; but she returned with the satisfaction, overcoming all the impulses of fear and remorse, that she had saved the object of her first and only love from ruin and flight.

But even then the reaction was on the spring;

the rebound was to be fearful and fatal. The teller at the bank had been struck with Effie's manner; and the non-counting of the notes had roused a suspicion, which fought its way even against the improbability of a mere girl perpetrating a crime from which females are generally free. He examined the draft, and soon saw that the signature was a bad imitation. Thereupon a messenger was despatched to Bristo Street for inquiry. John Carr, taken by surprise, declared that the draft, though written by the daughter, was forged — the forgery being in his own mind attributed to George Lindsay, his young salesman. Enough this for the bank, who had in the first place only to do with the utterer, against whom their evidence as yet only lay. Within a few hours afterwards Effie Carr was in the Tolbooth, charged with the crime of forging a cheque on her father's account-current.

The news soon spread over Edinburgh—at that time only an overgrown village, in so far as regarded local facilities for the spread of wonders. It had begun there, where the mother was in recurring faints, the father in distraction and not less mystery, George Lindsay in terror and pity. And here comes in the next strange turn of our story. Lindsay all of a sudden declared he was the person who imitated the name—a device of the yearning heart to save the girl of his affection from the gallows, and clutched at by the mother and father as a means of their daughter's redemption. One of those thinly-sown beings who are cold-blooded by nature, who take on love slowly but surely, and seem fitted to be martyrs, Lindsay defied all consequences, so that it might be that Effie Carr should escape an ignominious death. Nor did he take time for further deliberation; in less than half an hour he was in the procurator-fiscal's office; the willing self-criminator; the man who did the deed; the man who was ready to die for his young mistress and his love. His story, too, was as ready as it was truth-seeming. He declared that he had got Effie to write out the draft as if commissioned by John Carr; that he took it away, and with his own hands added the name; that he had returned the cheque to Effie to go with it to the bank, and had received the money from her on her return. The consequence was his wish, and it was inevitable. That same day George Lindsay was lodged also in the Tolbooth, satisfied that he had made a sacrifice of his life for one whom he had loved for years, and who yet had never shown him even a symptom of hope that his love would be returned.

All which proceedings soon came on the wings of rumour to the ears of Robert Stormonth, who was not formed to be a martyr even for a love which was to him as true as his nature would permit. He saw his danger, because he did not see the character of a faithful girl who would die rather than compromise her lover. He fled—aided probably by that very money he had wrung out of the hands of the devoted girl; nor was his disappearance connected with the tragic transaction; for, as we have said, the connexion between him and Effie had been kept a secret, and his flight could be sufficiently accounted for by his debt.

Meanwhile the precognitions or examination of the parties went on, and with a result as strange as it was puzzling to the officials. Effie was firm to her declaration that she not only wrote the body of the cheque, but attached to it the name of her father, and had appropriated the money in a way which she declined to state. On the other hand, Lindsay was equally stanch to his statement made to the procurator-fiscal, that he had got Effie to write the draft, had forged the name to it, and got the money from her. The authorities very soon saw that they had got more than the law bargained for or wanted; nor was the difficulty likely soon to be solved. The two parties could not both be guilty, according to the evidence, nor could one of them be guilty to the exclusion of the other; neither, when the balance was cast, was there much difference in the weight of the scales, because while it was in one view more likely that Lindsay signed the false name, it was beyond doubt that Effie wrote the body of the document, and she had moreover presented it. But was it for the honour of the law that people should be hanged on a likelihood? It was a new case without new heads to decide it, and it made no difference that the body of the people, who soon became inflamed on the subject, took the part of the girl and declared against the man. It was easy to be seen that the tracing of the money would go far to solve the mystery; and accordingly there was a strict search made in Lindsay's lodgings, as well as in Effie's private repositories at home. We need not say with what effect, where the money was over the Border and away. It was thus in all views more a case for Astræa than common heads; but then she had gone to heaven. The Lord Advocate soon saw that the law was likely to be caught in its own meshes. The first glimpse was got of the danger of hanging so versatile, so inconsistent, so unsearchable a creature as a human being on a mere confession of guilt. That that had been the law of Scotland in all time, nay, that it had been the law of the world from the beginning, there was no doubt. Who could know the murderer or the forger better than the murderer or the forger themselves? and would any one throw away his life on a false plea? The reasoning does not exhaust the deep subject; there remains the presumption that the criminal will, in ninety-nine cases out of a hundred, deny, and deny boldly. But our case threw a new light on the old law, and the Lord Advocate was slow to indict where he saw not only reasons for failure, but also rising difficulties which might strike at the respect upon which the law was founded.

The affair hung loose for a time; and Lindsay's friends, anxious to save him, got him induced to run his letters,—the effect of which is to give the prosecutor a period wherein to try the culprit, on failure of which the person charged is free. The same was done by Effie's father; but quickened as the Lord Advocate was, the difficulty still met him like a ghost that would not be laid,—that if he put Effie at the bar, Lindsay would appear in the witness-box; and if he put Lindsay on his trial, Effie would swear he was innocent; and as for two people forging *the same name*, the thing had never been heard of. And so it came to pass that the authorities at last, feeling they were in a cleft stick, where if they relieved one hand the other would be caught, were inclined to liberate both panels. But the bank was at that time preyed upon by forgeries, and were determined to make an example now when they had a culprit, or perhaps two. The consequence was, that the authorities were forced to give way, vindicating their right of choice as to the party they should arraign. That party was Effie Carr; and the choice justified itself by two considerations: that she, by writing and uttering the cheque, was so far committed by evidence exterior to her self-inculpation; and secondly, that Lindsay might break down in the witness-box under a searching examination. Effie was therefore indicted and placed at the bar. She pleaded guilty, but the prosecutor notwithstanding led evidence; and at length Lindsay appeared as a witness for the defence. The people who crowded the court had been aware from report of the condition in which Lindsay stood; but the deep silence which reigned throughout the hall when he was called to answer evinced the doubt whether he would stand true to his self-impeachment. The doubt was soon solved. With a face on which no trace of fear could be perceived, with a voice in which there was no quaver, he swore that it was he who signed the draft and sent Effie for the money. The oscillation of sympathy, which had for a time been suspended, came round again to the thin pale girl, who sat there looking wistfully and wonderingly into the face of the witness; and the murmuring approbation that broke out, in spite of the shrill "Silence" of the crier, expressed at once admiration of the man—criminal as he swore himself to be—and pity for the accused. What could the issue be? Effie was acquitted, and Lindsay sent back to gaol. Was he not to be tried? The officials felt that the game was dangerous. If Lindsay had stood firm in the box, had not Effie sat firm at the bar, with the very gallows in her eye; and would not she, in her turn, be as firm in the box? All which was too evident; and the consequence in the end came to be, that Lindsay was in the course of a few days set at liberty.

And now there occurred proceedings not less strange in the house of John Carr. Lindsay was turned off, because, though he had made a sacrifice of himself to save the life of Effie, the sacrifice was only that due to the justice he had offended. The dismissal was against the protestations of Effie, who alone knew he was innocent; and she had to bear the further grief of learning that Stormonth had left the city on the very day whereon she was apprehended — a discovery this too much for a frame always weak, and latterly so wasted by her confinement in prison, and the anguish of mind consequent upon her strange position. And so it came to pass, in a few more days, that she took to her bed, a wan, wasted, heart-broken creature; but stung as she had been by the conduct of the man she had offered to die to save, she felt even more the sting of ingratitude in herself for not divulging to her mother as much of her secret as would have saved Lindsay from dismissal; for she was now more and more satisfied that it was the strength of his love for her that had driven him to his great and perilous sacrifice. Nor could her mother, as she bent over her daughter, understand why her liberation should have been followed by so much of sorrow; nay, loving her as she did, she even reproached her as being ungrateful to God.

"Mother," said the girl, "I have a secret that lies like a stane upon my heart. George Lindsay had nae mair to do with that forgery than you."

"And who had to do with it then, Effie, dear?"

"Myself," continued the daughter; "I filled up the cheque at the bidding o' Robert Stormonth, whom I had lang loved. It was he wha put my faither's name to it. It was to him I gave the money, to relieve him from debt, and he has fled."

"Effie, Effie!" cried the mother; "and we have done this thing to George Lindsay—ta'en from him his basket and his store, yea, the bread o' his mouth, in recompense for trying to save your life by offering his ain."

"Yes, mother," added Effie; "but we must make that wrang richt."

"And mair, lass," rejoined the mother, as she

rose abruptly and nervously, and hurried to her husband, to whom she told the strange intelligence. Then John Carr was a just man as well as a loving parent; and while he forgave his unfortunate daughter, he went and brought back George Lindsay to his old place that very night; nor did he or Mrs Carr know the joy they had poured into the heart of the young man, for the reason that they did not know the love he bore to their daughter. But if this was a satisfaction to Effie, in so far as it relieved her heart of a burden, it brought to her a burden of another kind. The mother soon saw how matters stood with the heart of Lindsay, and she moreover saw that her or her daughter's gratitude could not be complete so long as he was denied the boon of being allowed to marry the girl he had saved from the gallows; and she waited her opportunity of breaking the delicate subject to Effie. It was not time yet, when Effie was an invalid; and even so far wasted and worn as to cause apprehensions of her ultimate fate, even death; nor perhaps would that time ever come when she could bear to hear the appeal without pain; for though Stormonth had ruined her character and her peace of mind—nay, had left her in circumstances almost unprecedented for treachery, baseness, and cruelty —he retained still the niche where the offerings of a first love had been made: his image had been indeed burned into the virgin heart, and no other form of man's face, though representing the possessor of beauty, wealth, and worldly honours, would ever take away that treasured symbol. It haunted her even as a shadow of herself, which, disappearing at sundown, comes again at the rise of the moon; nay, she would have been contented to make other sacrifices equally great as that which she had made; nor wild moors, nor streams, nor rugged hills, would have stopped her in an effort to look upon him once more, and replace that inevitable image by the real vision, which had first taken captive her young heart.

But time passed, bringing the usual ameliorations to the miserable. Effie got so far better in health that she became able to resume, in a languid way, her former duties, with the exception of those of "the gentle clerk"—for of these she had had enough; even the very look of a bank-draft brought a shudder over her; nor would she have entered the Bank of Scotland again, even with a good cheque for a thousand pounds to have been all her own. Meanwhile the patient George had plied a suit which he could only express by his eyes, or the attentions of one who worships; but he never alluded, even in their conversations, to the old sacrifice. The mother too, and not less the father, saw the advantages that might result as well to the health of her mind as that of her body. They had waited—a vain waiting—for the wearing out of the traces of the obdurate image: and when they thought they might take placidity as the sign of what they waited for, they first hinted, and then expressed in plain terms, the wishes of their hearts. For a time all their efforts were fruitless; but John Carr, getting old and weak, wished to be succeeded in his business by George; and the wife, when she became a widow, would require to be maintained, —reasons which had more weight with Effie than any others, excepting always the act of George's self-immolation at the shrine in which his fancy had placed her. The importunities at length wore out her resistings, without effacing the lines of the old and still endeared image; and she gave a cold, we may say reluctant, consent. The bride's "ay" was a sigh, the rapture a tear of sadness. But George was pleased even with this: Effie, the long-cherished Effie, was at length his.

In her new situation Effie Carr—now Mrs Lindsay—performed all the duties of a good and faithful wife; by an effort of the will no doubt, though in another sense only a sad obedience to necessity, of which we are all, as the creatures of motives, the very slaves. But the old image resisted the appeals of her reason, as well as the blandishments of a husband's love. She was only true, faithful, and kind, till the birth of a child lent its reconciling power to the efforts of duty. Some time afterwards John Carr died—an event which carried in its train the subsequent death of his wife. There was left to the son-in-law a dwindling business, and a very small sum of money; for the father had met with misfortunes in his declining years, which impaired health prevented him from resisting. Time wore on, and showed that the power of the martyr-spirit is not always that of the champion of worldly success; for it was now but a struggle between George Lindsay, with a stained name, and the stern demon of misfortune. He was at length overtaken by poverty, which, as affecting Effie, preyed so relentlessly upon his spirits, that within two years he followed John Carr to the grave. Effie was now left with two children to the work of her fingers, a poor weapon wherewith to beat off the wolf of want; and even this was curtailed by the effects of the old crime, which the public still kept in green remembrance.

Throughout, our story has been the sensationalism of angry Fate, and even less likely to be believed than the work of fiction. Nor was the vulture face of the Nemesis yet smoothed down. The grief of her bereavement had only partially diverted Effie's mind from the recollections of him who had ruined her, and yet could not be hated by her, nay, could not be but loved by her. The sensitised nerve, which had received the old image, gave it out fresh again to the reviving power of memory, and this was only a continuation of what had been a corroding custom of years and years. But as the saying goes, it is a long road that does not offer by its side the spreading bough of shade to the way-worn traveller. One day, when Effie was engaged with her work, of which she was as weary as of the dreaming which accompanied it, there appeared before her, without premonition or foreshadowing sign, Robert Stormonth, of Kelton, dressed as a country gentleman, booted, and with a whip in his hand.

"Are you Effie Carr?"

The question was useless to one who was already lying back in her chair in a state of unconsciousness, from which she recovered only to open her eyes and avert them, and shut them and open them again, like the victim of epilepsy.

"And do you fear me?" said the excited man, as he took her in his strong arms and stared wildly into her face; "I have more reason to fear you, whom I ruined," he continued. "Ay, brought within the verge of the gallows. I know it all, Effie. Open your eyes, dear soul, and smile once more upon me. Nay, I have known it for years, during which remorse has scourged me through the world. Look up, dear Effie, while I tell you I could bear the agony no longer; and now opportunity favours the wretched penitent, for my father is dead, and I am not only my own master, but master of Kelton, of which you once heard me speak. Will you not look up yet, dear Effie? I come to make amends to you, not by wealth merely, but to offer you again that love I once bore to you, and still bear. Another such look, dear; it is oil to my parched spirit. You are to consent to be my wife—the very smallest boon I dare offer."

During which strange rambling speech Effie was partly insensible; yet she heard enough to afford her clouded mind a glimpse of her condition, and of the meaning of what was said to her. For a time she kept staring into his face as if she had doubts of his real personality; nor could she find words to express even those more collected thoughts that began to gather into form.

"Robert Stormonth," at length she said, calmly, "and have you suffered too? Oh, this is more wonderful to me than a' the rest o' these wonderful things."

"As no man ever suffered, dear Effie," he answered. "I was on the eve of coming to you, when a friend I retained here wrote me to London of your marriage with the man who saved you from the fate into which I precipitated you. How I envied that man who offered to die for you! He seemed to take from me my only means of reparation; nay, my only chance of happiness. But he is dead. Heaven give peace to so noble a spirit! And now you are mine. It is mercy I come to seek in the first instance; the love—if that, after all that is past, is indeed possible—I will take my chance of that."

"Robert," cried the now weeping woman, "if that love had been aince less, what misery I would have been spared! Ay, and my father, and mother, and poor George Lindsay; a' helped awa to the grave by my crime, for it stuck to us to the end." And she buried her head in his bosom, sobbing piteously.

"*My* crime, dear Effie, not yours," said he. "It was you who saved my life; and if Heaven has a kindlier part than another for those who err by the fault of others, it will be reserved for one who made a sacrifice to love. But we have, I hope, something to enjoy before you go there, and as yet I have not got your forgiveness."

"It is yours—it is yours, Robert," was the sobbing answer. "Ay, and with it a' the love I ever had for you."

"Enough for this time, dear Effie," said he. "My horse waits for me. Expect me to-morrow at this hour with a better-arranged purpose." And folding her in his arms, and kissing her fervently, even as his remorse were thereby assuaged as well as his love gratified, he departed, leaving Effie to thoughts we should be sorry to think ourselves capable of putting into words. Nor need we say more than that Stormonth kept his word. Effie Carr was in a few days Mrs Stormonth, and in not many more the presiding female power in the fine residence of Kelton.

## The Story of Mary Mochrie and the Miracle of the Cod.

IT was said that David Hume's barber, who had the honour of shaving the philosopher every morning, was so scandalised by David's Essay on Miracles, that he told him to his face—which he was smoothing at the time—that Mary Mochrie's miracle shut his mouth. And no doubt this was so far true, for the shaver took care while he was telling the story to hold David's lips close with his left hand, while he was plying his razor with the other. David, we are informed, used to tell this anecdote himself along with the story of the modern miracle appended to it; and as the latter is a good example of the easy way by which the blind sentiment of wonder groping for light comes to refer strange things to Divine interposition, and consequently the facility of belief in those darker times, we may include among our stories for the amusement of our readers that of the miracle, which goes in this wise:—

On a fine day in the month of June a certain Miss Isabella Warrender, the daughter of a respectable burgess, bethought herself of the luxury of a plunge in the Forth, on the sands to the west of Newhaven, and with a view to safety, as well as companionship, she behoved to take with her her father's trusty servant, Mary Mochrie. The blue bathing-gowns were accordingly put into the basket, and away they went on their journey of two miles with heads "as light as lavrocks," and thinking of no other miracle in the world than that of enjoyment—a veritable miracle to many, insomuch as it is to them in this world of doubtful happiness and real misery miraculously scarce. Nor was it long, with their light feet, ere they reached their destination; all things, too, being otherwise propitious, for the sun was shining in a clear sky, the surface of the sea was as smooth as glass, and like a mirror reflected the rays of the sun; so that, to speak figuratively, Apollo and Neptune were on the best of terms, as if they had resolved to favour specially on that day so fair a specimen of an earthly maid, who, for a time, was to become a water nymph. So, after looking out from beneath her curls for Peeping Toms,—of whom, by the way, to the honour of Scotland, our Godivas in these parts have little to complain,—Isabella got herself made as like Musidora as possible, in which condition she remained only for that single moment occupied by Mary in investing her with the said blue gown. Whereupon, Mary having also divested herself of her clothes, was as quickly reclaimed from the searching eyes of the upper of the two propitious gods by her young mistress helping her on with her sea dress.

All which sacrifices to *Bona Dea* are pretty uniform, if we may not say that, although young women have as good a right to outrage modesty by splashing about perfectly nude in the sea as the men have, they know better than do any such naughty thing. Nor, perhaps, was it any exception, that as they went into the sea they took each other by the hand, just as Adam and Eve did when they walked hand in hand into a flood of sin, as enticing to them, too, as the shining water was to our virgins—a comparison more true than you may be at present thinking. Then having got up to the middle—that is, in a sense, half seas over, they got into that sportive mood which belongs to bathers, as if an infection from the playful element; and, of course, they could not avoid the usual ducking, which is performed by the two taking hold of both hands, and alternately or simultaneously dipping themselves over head, and as they emerge shaking their locks as the ducks do their wings when they come out of the water. All which was very pleasant, as might have been apparent from the laughing and screighing which terrified the Tom Norries there and then flying over their heads; but it so happened that in one of these see-saws Isabella's foot slipped, and the consequence was that her hands slipped also out of those of Mary, so that she fell back into the water, more afraid, of course, than hurt; nor was this all, for no sooner had Isabella got on her feet again than holding out her left hand she cried in rather a wild way that she had lost her ruby ring—nay, that very ring which a certain George Ballennie had given her as a pledge of his love, and the loss of which was so like an augury of evil. And then as it was Mary's hand which pulled it off, or rather Isabella's that left it in Mary's, it was natural she should ask at the same time whether Mary had it or had felt it, but Mary asserted that she had it not, neither had she felt it when coming off. So if Mary was honest it behoved to be in the sea, and in all likelihood would never be found again.

And thus the pleasant act of bathing was interrupted in the very middle, for how could there be any more splashing and tumbling and mermaiding with this terrible loss weighing upon Isabella's heart? She would not know how to face her mother; and as for Ballennie, might he not think that she who would not take better care of a love-token had no great love on her part to be betokened by a ring or anything else. The very sea which a moment before was as beautiful as a blushing bride holding out her arms for the embrace of the bridegroom, became as hateful to her as a Fury, and, hastening to the bank with tears in her eyes, which, of course, could not be seen, she began to dress. Mary, who seemed to participate in her young mistress's sorrow, commenced the same operation; but when the clothes were on what was to be done? The tide was ebbing, and an hour, or at most two, would discover the channel at the spot where the unlucky slip was made, but to remain all that time would produce uneasiness at home, and there appeared to be nothing for it but for the young lady to go to Edinburgh, and leave Mary to wait for the ebbing of the tide, and make a search among the shingle for the valuable article.

A plan accordingly carried out. Mary certainly awaited the ebb, and did make a search among the gravel, but whether that search was conducted in that assiduous way followed by those who are lighted in their travel by the Lamp of Hope, it is not for us at present to say. Certain at least it is that Mary did not seem very greatly disappointed at her failure in not finding Isabella's precious love-token, for which want of feeling we do not require to go very deep into Mary's breast, or any other body's breast, seeing she was a woman, and had a lover of her own, even George Gallie, as good as Ballennie any day. True, he had never given her a ruby ring; though, as for that, he would if he could, and if he couldn't how could he? So Mary was on a par with Isabella in that matter; still, we confess, she might have searched more carefully, unless, indeed, we are to be so ungallant as to believe that she had in her mind some foregone secret conclusion that the ring was not there to be found.

Nor, what is almost as strange, did Mary take up her basket and commence her journey homeward in that saddened way which belongs to deep disappointment. Nay, we are not sure but that the words of the old song of her whose ring had been stolen by a mermaid, were conned by Mary to herself as she trudged homewards,—

> "And sair she moiled, and sair she toiled,
> To find the ring lost in the sea,
> And still the thought within her wrought
> That she would never married be."

But there was something else in her head when she reached the house, where she met some very suspicious looks not only from Isabella, but also from Mrs Warrender, for we may as well confess that the daughter had told her mother that when the slip of the hand took place she felt as if the ring had been taken off by the hand of Mary. And then when Mary appeared with a lugubrious face, and reported that she had not found the ring in the shingle, the foresaid suspicion was so much confirmed, that very little more would be required to induce Mr Warrender to make some judicial investigation into the strange circumstance. An inauspicious afternoon and night for Mary, and not less the next day, when she was called into the dining-room, and so sharply interrogated by Mr Warrender, that she cried very bitterly, all the time asserting that she never felt her hand touch the ring, and that it had most certainly fallen into the water and been lost. But Mr Warrender was not a man who believed in tears, at least women's; for he was ungallant enough to think, that as we cannot distinguish *ex parte rei* between those of anger and those of sorrow, and as there is a kind called crocodile, as limpid as the others, and just as like a pretty dewdrop, so they never can or ought to be received as evidence either of guilt or innocence. And so it came about, that as the hours passed the conviction grew stronger and stronger in the minds of the family that the meek, and church-going, and psalm-singing Mary Mochrie was a thief.

Of this latter fact, in the peculiar circumstances

of the case, there could be no evidence beyond the finding of the missing article, either on Mary's person or in some place under her power, for Isabella's word could not go for much; and so it was resolved that Mary's person and trunk should be searched. A very strong step in the case of a girl who had hitherto held a very good character, and probably altogether unjustifiable, where so powerful an abstractor of earthly things as Neptune was apparently as much in the scrape as Mary. Yet this strong thing was done *illotis manibus*, and, as might have been expected, with no effect beyond scandalising Mary, who went so far as to say that Heaven took care of its own, and that God would in His own time and way show her persecutors that she was as innocent as that babe unborn, who takes away and places, nobody knows where, so many of the wickednesses of the world. But then an assertion of innocence in the grand style of an appeal to the Deity sometimes piques a prosecutor, because it conveys an imputation that the accused one is better taken care of by Heaven than he is; and so it turned out here, for Mr Warrender felt as if he had been challenged to the ultimate trial by ordeal, and he straightway proceeded to take measures for having Mary apprehended upon the charge of having robbed his daughter of the much-prized ring.

These measures were taken as they had been resolved upon, and here it behoves us, for a reason which may appear by and by, to be so particular as to say, that the officer was to come in the morning after breakfast to convey the alleged culprit to the office of the public prosecutor, for the purpose, in the first place, of examination. Nor was Mary unprepared, nay, she was not even to all appearance very much put about, for she had gone about her work as usual, and having finished what she had to do as maid-of-all-work — cook, scullery-maid, and scrub—she began to make preparations for cutting-up and gutting, and scraping, and washing the large cod, which lay upon the dresser ready for these operations, and which, by the way, Mrs Warrender had that morning, an hour before, bought for the sum of one and sixpence, from a Jenny Mucklebacket, of the village of Newhaven—another particular fact which we are bound to apologise for on the foresaid plea of necessity, lest we might incur the charge of wishing to produce an effect by Dutch painting. But Mary's services as to the cod were dispensed with by Mrs Warrender, if they were not actually resented as either a bribe to forego the prosecution, or a cold-blooded indifference assumed for the purpose of showing her innocence. And so when the officer came Mary was hurried away to undergo this terrible ordeal, which, whatever other effect it might have, could not fail to leave her marked with the very burning irons that might not inflict the punishment due to robbery.

Leaving Mrs Warrender with the cod, which is as indispensable to our legend as a frying-pan to a Dutch interior, or the bone of a pig to a saint's legend, we follow the prisoner to the office of the man who is a terror to evil-doers. Mr Warrender was there as the private prosecutor, and Isabella as a witness, or rather *the* witness. On being seated, the fiscal asked Mary, whether, on the day of the bathing, she had not seen the said ring on the finger of her young mistress; whereto Mary answered in the affirmative. Then came the application of the Lydian stone, in the form of the question, whether she did not, at the foresaid time and place, abstract the said ring from the finger of Isabella when she held her hand in the process of dipping; but Mary was here negative and firm, asserting that she did not, and giving emphasis to her denial by adding, that God knew she was as innocent as the foresaid babe. In spite of all which, Isabella insisted that she had been robbed in the manner set forth. The fiscal saw at once that the whole case lay between the two young women, and recommended Mr Warrender to let go the prosecution as one which must fail for defect of evidence;

but that gentleman, for the reason that he had so far committed himself, and also for that he was annoyed at what he called the impudence of a servant disputing the word of his daughter, and calling her, in effect, a liar, insisted upon his right, as the protector and curator of his daughter, of having the culprit committed to jail, in the expectation that, through some medium of the three magic balls, or otherwise, he would get more evidence of the crime. The fiscal had no alternative; and so Mary Mochrie was taken to the Tolbooth, with the ordinary result, in the first place, of the news going up and down the long street which then formed the city, that Mrs Warrender's servant was imprisoned for the strange crime of abstracting from Miss Warrender's finger, while bathing, the love-token given to her by her intended. There was, doubtless, about the tale just so much of romance that would serve it as wings to carry it wherever gossip was acceptable—and we would like to know where in that city it was not acceptable then, and where it is not acceptable now.

Meanwhile Mrs Warrender had been very busy with the mute person of our drama—the cod—in which, like the devil in the story who had bargained for a sinner and having got a saint instead, had half resolved to follow the advice of Burns and "take a thought and mend," she had got so much more than she bargained for with the fishwife that she was, when Mr Warrender and Isabella entered, ready to faint. They found her sitting in a chair scarcely able to move, under no less an agency than the fear of God. Her breath came and went with difficulty through lips with that degree of paleness which lips have a special tendency to take on, an expression of awe was over her face, and in her hand she held that identical ruby ring for the supposed theft of which the unfortunate Mary had been hurried to jail, and as for being able to speak she was as mute as the flounder in the proverb that never spoke but once; all she could do was to hold up the ring and point to the cod upon the dresser. But all in vain, for Mr Warrender could not see through the terrible mystery, nay, surely the most wonderful thing that had ever happened in this lower world since the time when the whale cast up Jonah just where and when he was wanted, till at length Mrs Warrender was enabled to utter a few broken words to the effect that the ring had been found in the stomach of the fish. Then, to be sure, all was plain enough—the cod was a chosen instrument in the hands of the great Author of Justice sent by a special message to save Mary Mochrie from the ruin which awaited her under a false charge. The conviction was easy in proportion to the charm which supernaturalism always holds over man—

> "True miracles are more believed
> The more they cannot be conceived;"

and we are to remember that the last witch had not been burnt at the time of our story. But what made this Divine interposition the more serious to the house of the Warrenders, the message from above was sent as direct as a letter by post, only not prepaid, for Mrs Warrender had paid for the fish; and so it was equally plain that a duty was thus put upon Mr Warrender of no ordinary kind.

Nor was he long in obeying the command. Taking the wonderful ring along with him he hurried away to the office he had so lately left, and told the miraculous tale to the man of prosecutions. And what although that astute personage smiled at the story, just as if he would have said, if he had thought it worth his while, "Was there any opportunity for Mary Mochrie handling the cod?"—it was only the small whipcord of scepticism applied to the posteriors of the rhinoceros of superstition, even that instinct in poor man to be eternally looking up into the blank sky for special providences. So Mr Warrender, now himself a holy instrument, got what he wanted—an order to the jailer for Mary's liberation. So away he went; and as he went to the Tolbooth he told every acquaintance he met the exciting story—among others his own clergyman of the Greyfriars, who held up his hands and said, " Wonderful are the ways of God ! Yea, this very thing hath a purpose in it, even that of utterly demolishing that arch sceptic David Hume's soul-destroying Essay on Miracles. I will verily take up the subject the next Sabbath." And thus, dropping the germs as he went, which formed a revolving radius line from the centre of the mystery—his own house—the consequence was that the miracle of the cod went like wildfire wherever there was the fuel of a predisposing superstition ; and where, we repeat, was that not then ? where is not now, despite of David with all his genius—the first and best of the anti-Positivists, because he was a true Pyrrhonean. Having got to the jail, Mr Warrender informed Mary of this wonderful turn of providence in her favour, whereat Mary, as a matter of course, held up her hands in great wonder and admiration.

But Mr Warrender was not, by this act of justice, yet done with Mary. It behoved him to take her home and restore her to her place, with a character not only cleared of all imputation, but illustrated by the shining light of the favour of Heaven ; and so he accompanied her down the thronged High Street,—an act which partook somewhat of the procession of a saint, whereat people stared ; nay, many who had heard of the miracle went up and shook hands with one who was the favourite of the

Great Disposer of events. Nor did her honours end with this display; for when they reached the house they found it filled with acquaintances, and even strangers, all anxious to see the wonderful fish, and the ring, and the maid. In the midst of all which honours Mary looked as simple as a Madonna; and if she winked it was only with one eye, and the winking was to herself. Even here her honours that day did not terminate, for she behoved for once to dine with the family—not on the cod, which was reserved as something sacred, like the small fishes offered by the Phaselites to their gods—but on a jolly leg of lamb, as a recompense for the breakfast of which she had that morning been deprived. Nay, as for the cod, in place of being eaten, it stood a risk of being pickled, and carried off to help the exchequer of some poor Catholic community in the land of miracles.

But probably the most wonderful part of our history consists in this fact, that no one ever hinted at the propriety of having recourse to the easiest and most natural way of solving a knot so easily tied; but we have only to remember another mysstery—that of the gullibility of man when under the hunger of superstition. Nor need we say that the maw of a cod, big and omnivorous as it is, never equalled that of the miracle-devourer's, possessing, as it does, too, the peculiarity of keeping so long that which is accepted. Wherein it resembles the purse of the miser, the click of the spring of which is the sign of perpetual imprisonment. We only hear the subsequent jingle of the coin, and the jingle in our present instance might have lasted for twenty years, during all which time Mary Mochrie's miracle might have served as the best answer to the Essay of the renowned sceptic.

And thus we are brought back to the anecdote with which we set out. The story we have told is, in all its essentials, that which Donald Gorm, David Hume's barber, treated him to on that morning when he wanted to close up for ever the mouth of the arch sceptic. It is not easy to smile while under the hands of a story-telling barber, for the reason that the contracted muscle runs a risk of being still more contracted by a slice being taken off it by a resolute razor moving in straight lines, so that probably it was not till Donald had finished both the story and the shaving, that David dared to indulge in that good-natured smile with which he used to meet his opponents, even in the teeth of the Gael's oath, "'Tis a miracle, py Cot,"—a word this latter which, in Donald's humour, might stand for the word cod, as well as for another too sacred to be here mentioned.

Yet the philosopher had further occasion for his

good-humoured reticence, with which, as is well known, he declared he would alone meet the censors of his Essay, for it was really on the occasion of this great religious sensation in the city that the washer-women at the "Nor' Loch" threatened to "dook him," for the reason that, as they had heard, he had not only written that detestable Essay to prove that no miracles (for they were ungenerous enough to pay no attention to his *very* grave exception of the real Bible ones) could ever be, but he had actually gone the extreme length of disbelieving the intervention of God to save the innocent Mary Mochrie from the Moloch of the criminal law. We need not be unassured that this additional bit of gossip, as it spread though the city, would only tend to the inflammation that already prevailed. Nor need we wonder at all this, when we remember the play of metaphysical wit, which was received as very serious by the vulgar,—that David believed in nothing, except that there was no God.

But the mind of the Edinburgh public was not destined to cool down before it underwent further combustion. It happened that a certain person of the name of Gallie, a common working jeweller in World's End Close, was possessed of knowledge which he had picked up on the road to Newhaven, whither he had been going to bathe, on that very morning when the miraculous ring was lost, and which knowledge, he thought, being a knowing fellow, he could turn to account in the midst of the heat of collision between the miracle-mongers and the sceptics, even as he might have transmuted by the fire of the furnace a piece of base metal into gold; and he took a strange way to effect his purpose. Having first called on Mr Warrender and got a sight of the magic ring, he next wrote an advertisement, which he got printed in the form of the small posters of that day of Lilliputian bills. It ran in these terms:—" Mary Mochrie's Miracle.— If any one is anxious to learne the trew secret of this reputyd miracle, let him or her, mann or woman, hye to the closs of ye Warld's End, where Michael Gallie resideth, and on ye payement of one shilling they will hear somethyng that will astonie them; but not one to tell ye other upon his aith."

Copies of this bill Gallie posted on several walls in the most crowded parts of the city, and the consequence was such a crowd at World's End Close as might have been looked for if the close had really been the last refuge from a conflagration of another kind. The applicants got their turn of entry; every one came out with a face expressive of wonder, yet so true were they to their oath, that no one would tell a word he had heard behind the veil of Gallie's mystery, so that the curiosity of the outsiders, who wanted to save their shillings, became inflamed by pique in addition to curiosity. The secret took on the sacred and cabalistic character of a mystery, and the mystery feeding, as it always does, upon whispers and ominous looks, increased as the hours passed. Nor can we wonder at an excitement which had religion at the bottom of it, and the vanquishment of the soul-destroying David for the fruitful and ultimate issue. It was only the high price of admission which limited the number of Gallie's shillings, for during the entire day the stern obligation of an oath proved the stern honesty of a religious people. It was said—and I see no reason to doubt the truth of the report—that Dr Robertson and many others of the educated classes caught the infection and paid their shilling; but we may doubt if the imperturbable David would risk his body or trouble his spirit by looking into the mysterious close of the World's End.

As to what took place within Gallie's room, it would seem that the ingenious fellow, when he saw the heather on fire, set his gins for the hares and conies in such a way as to catch them by dozens. He allowed the room to fill, and having administered the oath to two or three dozen at a time, he contrived during the course of the day to bag more shillings than there might have been supposed to be fools or religious enthusiasts even in superstitious Edinburgh. Afterwards, when rumour became busy with his gains, it was said that he was thereby enabled to set up the famous silversmith's shop that so long, under the name of "Gallie and Son," occupied a prominent front in the High Street, between Halkerston's Wynd and Milne's Entry.

But as all things that depend upon mere human testimony must ultimately be left insoluble, except as belief makes an election and decision, so even the revelation of the prophet Gallie did not settle the great question of Mochrie *versus* Hume, for Gallie could offer no corroboration of the testimony of which he contrived to make a little fortune. That revelation came to be known very well the next day, probably from the softening and tongue-loosening influence of Edinburgh ale exercised upon even gnarled and cross-grained Presbyterians; and we need be under no doubt that Donald Gorm, when he shaved the philosopher next morning, was in full possession of the secret, though we might be entitled to hold pretty fast by the suspicion that he would not court another smile from David by recounting to him the destruction of his, Donald's, theory of the miracle.

With an apology for having kept the reader too

long from a knowledge of Gallie's revelation, we now proceed to give it as it was currently reported. It seemed that on that morning when the two girls went to bathe, Gallie had left Edinburgh for the same purpose about an hour later—a statement probable enough, although not attempted to be supported by any evidence. When about halfway on his journey, he met Mary Mochrie, who, strangely enough, though perfectly true, was his sweetheart. After some talk about the kind of bathe she had had, Mary showed him a ring, which she said she had bought from an old Jew broker on the previous day, and which she regretted was too wide for her finger. She then asked him to take it home with him and reduce it. Gallie having taken the ring into his hand started the moment he fixed his eye upon it.

"That ring," said he, for, notwithstanding his scheme to make capital out of superstition, of which he was an enemy, he was an honest fellow,—"that ring belongs to your young mistress; and the reason I know this is that I fixed the ruby in it for her not yet a fortnight since."

Taken thus aback, Mary began to prevaricate, saying that Miss Isabella Warrender had given it to her.

"That cannot be," said Gallie, "because she told

me it was a present from her lover, George Ballennie, to whom she is to be married."

Words which Gallie uttered in a solemn if not sorrowful tone, and a look indicating displeasure and disappointment at thus detecting in the woman whom he had intended to marry, both theft and falsehood. Nor were these words left unrequited, for the fiery girl, snatching the ring out of his hand, called him a liar, besides taunting him with a certain pendulous attitude which his father, old Gallie, had assumed somewhere about the precincts of the Tolbooth immediately before dying. The cruel remark was one of those combinations of sharp words which have a tendency to stick, especially where the brain to which they adhere has been previously occupied by love, and so Gallie, muttering to himself a determination to be revenged, parted from her for ever, and proceeded on his way to Newhaven.

Things in this world being so arranged that one person's misfortune or wretchedness becomes another person's opportunity, we may see how Gallie came to his purpose. Perhaps he might not have thought it worth his pains to expose his own sweetheart from a mere feeling of revenge, but when he came to find that the woman who had cast up to him his father's misfortune, had taken or been put into the position of an instrument of God's grace, that the public had been by her precipitated into a superstitious enthusiasm—a species of feeling which he hated, (for who knows but that he might have been descended from that older Gallio who deserved to have been hanged?) and that he saw by the clear vision of ingenuity that he could revenge himself as to Mary, and make himself rich at the expense of the fools whom he despised, he fell upon the adroit scheme which we have so faithfully recorded.

We have already also said that the oath of secrecy which Gallie had imposed on his dupes was dispensed with by some of the "loose-fish" who could not be so easily caught as the devout cod. But this did not end the controversy, for it immediately took the form of a contest between the Gallieites and the Mochricites, and the fury of the contest having drawn the attention of the officials of the law, Mary was again apprehended, with the view to be indicted for the theft of the ring, provided any corroborative testimony could be got in support of the statement of Gallie, who was forced to make his revelation to the fiscal, this one time without a shilling. The Scotch people are blessed or cursed with a metaphysical tendency, and this may be the reason of their peculiar faith, as well as of their old suspicion of human testimony in the courts of law. One witness has never been received in Scotland as good for anything, if standing alone ; and when we look to the samples of humanity that meet us every day, so nicely poised between truth and falsehood, that the weight of a Queen Anne's farthing would decide the inclination to the one side or the other, we are apt to think our judges rather sagacious. Perhaps they thought of themselves in these palmy days when they took bribes, and considered them very good and gracious things, too, in their own way. But be all that as it may, the evidence of Gallie was not corroborated in any way; the ring might have been put into the cod's mouth by Isabella Warrender herself to ruin Mary. Woman can do such things; and Gallie's accusation might have been the consequence of Mary's allusion to the fate of his father. The result, accordingly, was, that Mary Mochrie was dismissed. Yet even here the affair did not end, for some people received her with open arms, as being a vessel of mercy.

## The Story of the Pelican.

THOUGH not so much a tradition as a memory still fresh probably in the minds of some of the good old Edinburgh folks, we here offer, chiefly for the benefit of our young female readers who are fond of a story wherein little heroines figure, as in Béranger's "Sylphide," an account of a very famous adventure of a certain little Jeannie Deans in our city—the more like the elder Jeannie, inasmuch as they both were concerned in a loving effort to save the life of a sister. Whereunto, as a very necessary introduction, it behoves us to set forth that there was, some sixty years ago, more or less, a certain Mr William Maconie, who was a merchant on the South Bridge of Edinburgh, but who, for the sake of exercise and fresh air,—a commodity this last he need not have gone so far from the Calton Hill to seek—resided at Juniper Green, a little village three or four miles from St Giles's. Nor did this distance incommode him much, seeing that he had the attraction to quicken his steps homewards of a pretty young wife and two little twin daughters, Mary and Annie, as like each other as two rosebuds partially opened, and as like their mother, too, as the objects of our simile are to themselves when full blown.

Peculiar in this respect of having twins at the outset, and sisters too — a good beginning of a contract to perpetuate the species—Mr Maconie was destined to be even more so, inasmuch as there came no more of these pleasant *deliciæ domi*, at least up to the time of our curious story — a circumstance the more to be regretted by the father in consequence of a strange fancy (never told to his wife) that possessed him of wishing to insure the lives of his children as they came into the world, or at least after they had got through the rather uninsurable period of mere infant life. And in execution of this fancy—a very fair and reasonable one, and not uncommon at that time, whatever it may be now, when people are not so provident—he had got an insurance to the extent of five hundred pounds effected in the Pelican Office—perhaps the most famous at that time—on the lives of the said twins, Mary and Annie, who were, no doubt, altogether unconscious of the importance they were thus made to hold in the world.

Yet, unfortunately for the far-seeing and provident father, this scheme threatened to fructify sooner than he wished, if indeed it could ever have fructified to his satisfaction; for the grisly spectre of Typhus laid his relentless hand upon Mary when she—and of a consequence Annie—was somewhere about eight years old. And surely, being as we are very hopeful optimists in the cause of human nature, we need not say that the father, as he and his wife watched the suffering invalid on through the weary days and nights of the progress towards the crisis of that dangerous ailment, never once thought of the Pelican, except as a bird that feeds its young with the warm blood of its breast. But, sorrowful as they were, their grief was nothing in comparison with the distress of little Annie, who slipped about listening and making all manner of anxious inquiries about her sick sister, whom she was prohibited from seeing for fear of her being touched by the said spectre; nor was her heart the less troubled with fears for her life, that all things seemed so quiet and mysterious about the house— the doctor coming and going, and the father and mother whispering to each other, but never to her, and their faces so sad-like and mournful, in place of being, as was their wont, so cheerful and happy.

And surely all this solicitude on the part of Annie Maconie need not excite our wonder, when we consider that, from the time of their birth, the twin sisters had never been separated; but that, from the moment they had made their entrance on this world's stage, they had been always each where the other was, and had run each where the other ran, wished each what the other wished, and wept and laughed each when the other wept or laughed. Nature, indeed, before it came into her fickle head to make two of them, had, in all probability, intended these little sisters—" little cherries on one stalk"—to be but one; and they could only be said not to be *one*, because of their bodies being two—a circumstance of no great importance, for, in spite of the duality of body, the spirit that animated them was a unity, and as we know from an old philosopher called Plato, the spirit is really the human creature, the flesh and bones constituting the body being nothing more than a mere husk intended at the end to feed worms. And then the mother helped this sameness by dressing them so like each other, as if she wanted to make a " Comedy of Errors " out of the two little female Dromios.

But in the middle of this mystery and solicitude, it happened that Annie was to get some light; for at breakfast one morning—not yet that of the expected crisis—when her father and mother were talking earnestly in an undertone to each other, all unaware that the child, as she was moving about, was watching their words and looks, much as an older victim of credulity may be supposed to hang on the cabalistic movements and incantations of a sibyl, the attentive little listener eagerly drank in every word of the following conversation:—

"The doctor is so doubtful," said the anxious mother, with a tear in her eye, "that I have scarcely any hope; and if she is taken away, the very look of Annie, left alone 'bleating for her sister lamb,' will break my heart altogether."

"Yes," rejoined Mr Maconie, "it would be hard to bear; but,"—and it was the first time since Mary's illness he had ever remembered the insurance,—"it was wise that I insured poor Mary's life in the Pelican."

"Insured her life in the Pelican!" echoed the wife, in a higher tone. "That was at least lucky; but, oh! I hope we will not need to have our grief solaced by that comfort in affliction for many a day."

And this colloquy had scarcely been finished when the doctor entered, having gone previously into the invalid's room, with a very mournful expression upon his face; nor did his words make that expression any more bearable, as he said—

"I am sorry to say I do not like Mary's appearance so well to-day. I fear it is to be one of those cases where we cannot discover anything like a crisis at all; indeed, I have doubts about this old theory being applicable to this kind of fever, where the virus goes on gradually working to the end."

"The end!" echoed Mrs Maconie; "then, doctor, I fear you see what that will be."

"I would not like to say," added he; "but I fear you must make up your mind for the worst."

Now, all this was overheard by Annie, who, we may here seize the opportunity of saying, was, in addition to being a sensitive creature, one of those precocious little philosophers thinly spread in the female world, and made what they are often by delicate health, which reduces them to a habit of thinking much before their time. Not that she wanted the vivacity of her age, but that it was tempered by periods of serious musing, when all kinds of what the Scotch call "auld farrent" (far yont) thoughts come to be where they should not be, the consequence being a weird-like kind of wisdom, very like that of the aged; so the effect on a creature so constituted was just equal to the cause. Annie ran out of the room with her face concealed in her hands, and got into a small bedroom darkened by the window-blind, and there, in an obscurity and solitude suited to her mind and feelings, she resigned herself to the grief of the young heart. It was now clear to her that her dear Mary was to be taken from her; had not the doctor said as much? And then she had never seen death, of which she had read and heard and thought so much, that she looked upon it as a thing altogether mysterious and terrible. But had she not overheard her father say that he had insured poor dear Mary's life with the Pelican? and had she not heard of the pelican—yea, the pelican of the wilderness—as a creature of a most mythical kind, though she knew not aught of its nature, whether bird or beast, or man or woman, or angel. But whatever it might be, certain it was that her father would never have got this wonderful creature to insure Mary's life if it was not possessed of the power to bring about so great a result; so she cogitated, and mused, and philosophised in her small way, till she came to the conclusion that the pelican not only had the destiny of Mary in its hands, but was under an obligation to save her from that death which was so terrible to her. Nor had she done yet with the all-important subject; for all at once it came into her head as a faint memory, that one day, when her father was taking her along with her mother through the city, he pointed to a gilded sign, with a large bird represented thereon tearing its breast with its long beak and letting out the blood to its young, who were holding their mouths open to drink it in. "There," said he, "is the Pelican;" words she remembered even to that hour, for they were imprinted upon her mind by the formidable appearance of the wonderful-looking creature feeding its young with the very blood of its bosom. But withal she had sense enough to know—being, as we have said, a small philosopher—that a mere bird, however endowed with the power of sustaining the lives of its offspring, could not save that of her sister, and therefore it behoved to be only the symbol of some power within the office over the door of which the said sign was suspended. Nor in all this was Annie Maconie more extravagant than are nineteen-twentieths of the thousand millions in the world who still cling to occult causes.

And with those there came other equally strange thoughts; but beyond all she could not for the very life of her comprehend that most inexcusable apathy of her father, who, though he had heard with his own ears, from good authority, that her beloved Mary was lying in the next bed-room dying, never seemed to think of hurrying away to town—even to that very pelican who had so generously undertaken to insure Mary's life. It was an apathy unbecoming a father; and the blood of her little heart warmed with indignation at the very time that the said heart was down in sorrow as far as its loose strings would enable it to go. But was there no remedy? To be sure there was, and Annie knew, moreover, what it was; but then it was to be got only by a sacrifice, and that sacrifice she also knew, though it must of necessity be kept in the meantime as secret as the wonderful doings in the death-chamber of the palace of a certain Bluebeard.

Great thoughts these for so little a woman as Annie Maconie; and no doubt the greatness and the weight of them were the cause why, for all that day—every hour of which her father was allowing to pass—she was more melancholy and thoughtful than she had ever been since Mary began to be ill. But, somehow, there was a peculiar change which even her mother could observe in her; for while she had been in the habit of weeping for her sister, yea, and sobbing very piteously, she was all this day apparently in a reverie. Nor even up to the time of her going to bed was she less thoughtful and abstracted, even as if she had been engaged in solving some problem great to her, however small it might seem to grown-up infants. As for sleeping under the weight of so much responsibility, it might seem to be out of the question, and so verily it was; for her little body, acted on by the big thoughts, was moved from one side to another all night, so that she never slept a wink, still thinking and thinking, in her unutterable grief, of poor Mary, her father's criminal passiveness, and that most occult remedy which so completely engrossed her mind.

But certainly it was the light of morning for which sister Annie sighed; and when it came glinting in at the small window, she was up and beginning to dress, all the while listening lest the servant or any other one in the house should know she was up at that hour. Having completed her toilet, she slipped downstairs, and having got to the lobby, she was provident enough to lay hold of an umbrella, for she suspected the elements as being in league against her. Thus equipped, she crept out by the back-door, and having got thus free, she hurried along, never looking behind her till she came to the main road to Edinburgh, when she mounted the umbrella—one used by her father, and so large that it was more like a main-sheet than a covering suitable to so small a personage; so it behoved, that if she met any other "travellers on purpose bent," the moving body must have appeared to be some small tent on its way to a fair, carried by the proprietor thereof, of whom no more could be seen but the two short toddling legs, and the hem of the black riding-hood. But what cared Annie? She toiled along; the miles were long in comparison of the short legs, but then there was a large purpose in that little body, in the view of which miles were of small account, however long a time it might take those steps to go over them. Nor was it any drawback to all this energy, concentrated in so small a bulk, that she had had no breakfast. Was the dying sister Mary able to take any breakfast? and why should Annie eat when Mary, who did all she did—and she always did everything that sister Mary did—could not? The argument was enough for our little logician.

By the time she reached, by those short steps of hers, the great city, it was half-past eleven, and she had before her still a great deal to accomplish. She made out, after considerable wanderings, the street signalised above all streets by that wonderful bird; but after she got into it, the greater difficulty remained of finding the figure itself, whereto there was this untoward obstacle, that it was still drizzling in the thick Scotch way of concrete drops of mist, and the umbrella which she held over her head was so large that no turning it aside would enable her to see under the rim at such an angle as would permit her scanning so elevated a position, and so there was nothing for it but to draw it down. But even this was a task —heavy as the main-sheet was with rain, and rattling in a considerable wind—almost beyond her strength; and if it hadn't been that a kindly personage who saw the little maid's difficulty gave her assistance, she might not have been able to accomplish it. And now, with the heavy article in her hand, she peered about for another half-hour, till at length her gladdened eye fell upon the mystic symbol.

And no sooner had she made sure of the object, than she found her way into the office, asking the porter as well as a clerk where the pelican was to be found—questions that produced a smile; but smile here or smile there, Annie was not to be beat, nor did she stop in her progress until at last she was shown into a room where she saw perched on a high stool with three (of course) long legs, a strange-looking personage with a curled wig and a pair of green spectacles, who no doubt must be the pelican himself. As she appeared in the room, with the umbrella, not much shorter or less in circumference than herself, the gentleman looked curiously at her, wondering no doubt what the errand of so strange a little customer could be.

"Well, my little lady," said he, "what may be your pleasure?"

"I want the pelican," said Annie.

The gentleman was still more astonished, even to the extent that he laid down his pen and looked at her again.

"The pelican, dear?"

"Ay; just the pelican," answered she, deliberately, and even a little indignantly. "Are you the pelican?"

"Why, yes, dear; all that is for it below the figure," said he, smiling, and wondering what the next question would be.

"I am so glad I have found you," said she; "because sister Mary is dying."

"And who is sister Mary?"

"My sister, Mary Maconie, at Juniper Green."

Whereupon the gentleman began to remember that the name of William Maconie was in his books as holder of a policy.

"And what more?"

"My father says the pelican insured Mary's life, and I want you to come direct and do it, because I couldn't live if Mary were to die. And there's no time to be lost."

"Oh! I see, dear; and who sent you?"

"Nobody," answered Annie. "My father wouldn't come to you, and I have come from Juniper Green myself, without telling my father or mother."

"Oh yes, dear; I understand you."

"But you must do it quick," continued she, "because the doctor says she's in great danger; so you must come with me, and save her immediately."

"I am sorry, my dear little lady," rejoined he,

"that I cannot go with you; but I will set about it immediately, and I have no doubt, being able to go faster than you, that I will get there before you, so that all will be right before you arrive."

"See that you do it, then," said she, "because I can't live if Mary dies. Are you quite sure you will do it?"

"Perfectly sure, my little dear," added he; "go away home, and all will be right. The pelican will do his duty."

And Annie being thus satisfied, went away, dragging the main-sheet after her, and having upon her face a look of contentment, if not absolute happiness, in place of the sorrow which had occupied it during all the time of her toilsome journey. The same road is to be retraced; and if she had an object before which nerved her little limbs, she had now the delightful consciousness of that object having been effected—a feeling of inspiration which enabled her, hungry as she was, to overcome all the toil of the return. Another two hours, with that heavy umbrella overhead as well as body, brought her at length home, where she found that people had been sent out in various directions to find the missing Annie. The mother was in tears, and the father in great anxiety; and no sooner had she entered and laid down her burden, than she was clasped to the bosom, first of one parent, and then of the other.

"But where is the pelican?" said the anxious little maid.

"The pelican! my darling," cried the mother; "what do you mean?"

"Oh! I have been to him at his own office at Edinburgh, to get him to come and save Mary's life, and he said he would be here before me."

"And what in the world put it in your head to go there?" again asked the mother.

"Because I heard my father say yesterday that the pelican had insured dear sister Mary's life, and I went to tell him to come and do it immediately; because, if Mary were to die, I couldn't live, you know—that's the reason, dear mother."

"Yes, yes," said the father, scarcely able to repress a smile which rose in spite of his grief. "I see it all; you did a very right thing, my love. The pelican has been here, and Mary is better."

"Oh! I am so glad," rejoined Annie, "for I wasn't sure whether he had come or not; because, though I looked for him on the road, I couldn't see him."

At the same moment the doctor came in, with a blithe face.

"Mary is safe now," said he. "There has been a crisis, after all. The sweat has broken out upon her dry skin, and she will be well in a very short time."

"And there's no thanks to you," said Annie, "because it was I who went for the pelican."

Whereupon the doctor looked to the father, who, taking him aside, narrated to him the story, at which the doctor was so pleased that he laughed right out.

"You're the noblest little heroine I ever heard of," said he.

"But have you had anything to eat, dear, in this long journey?" said the mother.

"No, I didn't want," was the answer; "all I wanted was to save Mary's life, and I am glad I have done it."

And glad would we be if, by the laws of historical truth, our stranger story could have ended here; but, alas! we are obliged to pain the good reader's heart by saying that the demon who had left the troubled little breast of Mary Maconie took possession of Annie's. The very next day she lay extended on the bed, panting under the fell embrace of the relentless foe. As Mary got better, Annie grew worse; and her case was so far unlike Mary's, that there was more a tendency to a fevered state of the brain. The little sufferer watched with curious eyes the anxious faces of her parents, and seemed conscious that she was in a dangerous condition. Nor did it fail to occur to her as a great mystery as well as wonder, why they did not send for the wonderful being who had so promptly saved the life of her sister. The thought haunted her, yet she was afraid to mention it to her mother, because it implied a sense of danger—a fear which one evening she overcame. Fixing her eyes, now every moment waxing less clear, on the face of her mother—

"Oh! mother, dear," she whispered, "why do you not send for the pelican?"

In other circumstances the mother would have smiled; but, alas, no smile could be seen on that pale face. Whether the pelican was sent for we know not, but certain it is, that he had no power to save poor Annie, and she died within the week. But she did not die in vain, for the large sum insured upon her life eventually came to Mary, whom she loved so dearly.

## The Story of Davie Dempster's Ghaist.

THERE was once an old saying very common in the mouths of the Edinburgh people—"As dead as Davie Dempster." It has long since passed away; but whether it was preferable to the one to which it has given place, viz.,—"As dead as a door-nail," we must leave to those wise people who can measure degrees of non-vitality in objects which are without life. Be all which as it may, the imputed deadness of David Dempster may appear to have some interest to us when we know the story from which the old popular saying took its rise; and the more, that the story cannot be said to want a moral vitality, if it has not even a spice of humour in it. Certain, to begin with, David Dempster was at least once alive, for we can vouch for his having been a very respectable denizen of the old city. We can even impart the nature of his calling, that of a trafficker in the stuff of man's wearing apparel, which he sold to those who were willing to buy, and even to some who were unwilling to buy; for David's tongue, if not so long as his ell-wand, was a deuced deal more supple. Nor does our information end here, for we can, we are happy to say, tell the name of his wife, which was Dorothy; nay, we know even the interesting particular, that when David had more Edinburgh ale in his stomach than humility in his head, he got so far into the heroics as to call her Dorothea; but as for the maiden name of this woman, who was the wife of a man so famous as to have been the source and origin of a proverb, we regret to say that it has gone into the limbo of things that are lost. To make amends, we can, however, add that Mrs Dempster was, at the time of our story, as plump and well coloured as Florabel; but as for David, who was ten years older than his wife, he was just as plain as any man needs be without pretension to being disagreeable.

We have said that David Dempster and his wife were respectable, and we do not intend to offer a jot more evidence on the point, than the fact that they went to "the kirk" on Sundays, and that, too, with faces of the normal Calvinistic elongation, and in good clothes; Dorothy being covered, head and all, with her red silk plaid, and David immersed in the long square coat of the times, with cuffs as big as four-pound tea-bags, buttons as broad as crown-pieces, and pockets able to have held Dr

Webster's—their minister's—pulpit Bible in the one, and as many bottles of wine as the worthy gentleman could carry away at a sitting, in the other; an allusion this last by no means ill-natured, as we may show by making the admission that, if David and Dorothy had had heads big enough to carry away all that their excellent preacher told them, they required no more for unction and function for a whole week. But, however fair things looked in the sanctuary, it was otherwise at home in Lady Stair's Close, where they resided, for it so happened that our worthy clothes-merchant had got into debt; nay, there were hornings and captions out against him, and he stood a chance any day in all the year round of being shut up in "The Heart of Mid-Lothian," not nearly so soft a one as Dorothy's. Not that all David's creditors were equally hard upon him, for the laird of Rubbledykes—a small property on the left-hand side of the road to Cramond—Mr Thomas Snoddy, who had lent him two hundred pounds Scots, never asked him for a farthing; the reason of which requires a little explanation.

In real secret truth the laird had been a lover of Dorothy's before she was married to David, and there is no doubt that if he had declared himself, with Rubbledykes to back him, he would have carried off the adorable Dorothy in triumph; but then

R

it was the laird's misfortune to be what the Scotch call "a blate lover;" which is just to say, a belated one; and Dorothy was married to the spruce and ardent David before she knew that a real laird of an estate was dying in secret for her. Nor could she have had any doubt of the fact, for Mr Snoddy summoned up courage to tell her so himself—a circumstance which cost him something, insomuch as no sooner did David know the fact than he asked him for the loan of the said two hundred pounds Scots money. Of course, David being, as we have said, a man with a supple tongue, and brains at the end of it, knew what he was about, and so sure enough he succeeded; for Rubbledykes, who would not have lent two hundred pound Scots to the treasurer of the Virgin Mary on a note-of-hand, payable in Heaven, was even delighted to advance that sum to the husband of his once loved, and for ever lost, Dorothy. And in this act the laird was wonderfully liberal; for in his secret heart he conditioned for no more than the liberty of being allowed to visit the house in Lady Stair's Close on market days, and sit beside Dorothy, and look at her, and wonder at her still red cheeks—albeit, more of the pickling cabbage than the rose—and sigh at the loss of such a treasure. Neither in suffering all this adoration did Mrs Dempster commit any very heinous sin; nay, being, as a good Calvinist, a believer in the excellent doctrine (if acted up to) of "total depravity," she was necessarily in the highway of salvation.

Neither did Mrs Dempster think it necessary to conceal any of these doings from David. Nay, on one particular Wednesday, after the laird had had his fill of this will-worship, she brought the subject up in so particular a way to her husband, that we are thereby led to believe that they understood each other, and could act in concert. The occasion was the complaint of David that some of his other creditors were likely to be down upon him.

"Ah, Dorothy, if they were a' like Snoddy."

Not a very respectful way of alluding to no less a personage than the laird of Rubbledykes, let alone his kindness; but then David, being a debtor, did not respect himself, and nothing was ever more true than the saying, "That our own self-respect is the foundation of that respect which we pay to others."

"But they're *no'* a' like the laird," replied Dorothy; "and what's mair, David, my man, the laird winna be ane o' your creditors lang either."

"What mean you, lass?" inquired David.

"I just mean neither mair nor less than that Thomas Snoddy o' Rubbledykes, wha should hae been my gudeman, is deein' as fast as he can bicker; and that by and by I might have been my Leddy

Rubbledykes wi' three hundred a year, and nae husband to trouble me."

"That's ill news," continued David; "for if he dees, the debt will gae to his brother, a man who would raze the skin frae the mother's face that bore him, if he could mak a leather purse out o't. But what maks ye think he is deein', lass?"

"Deein'!" rejoined Dorothy, with an ill-timed, if not cruel laugh. "That cough o' his would kill baith you and me in a year, even if we should only cough time about."

"Ower true, I fear," groaned David; "and then there's a' thae ither debts upon me. Hark, Dorothy, ye're a clever dame; could ye no' get the laird to discharge the debt?"

"Maybe I might, were I to kiss him, David," was the answer, with another smile.

"And what for no'?" asked this honest man, who raised his voice in the Tron every Sunday.

"Because I am neither a Judith nor a Judas," replied she.

"But ye're a Christian," was the ready rejoinder; "and what's mair, a Calvinist."

"As if a body could be a Christian without being a Calvinist," said she. "But what do ye mean, David—are ye crazy? Why should I kiss another man because I'm a Calvinist?"

"Nae sin, nae salvation," said he.

Whereupon the worthy couple laughed at a tenet which, being liable to a double construction, has always been dangerous to the common people of Scotland. And what was worse, this laugh was only the prelude to a further conversation so deep and mysterious, and withal conducted in so low a train of whispers and re-whispers, that even our familiar, endowed as he is with the power of going through stone walls, could carry off no more than smiles and nods and winks, and more and more of the same kind of laughs. But as the son of Sirach says, "There is an exquisite subtlety, and the same is unjust;" and "Wrath will surely search it." Nor was there in this case much time required for the retribution, for the very next day a man rushed into the house of Mrs Dempster with the intelligence on his tongue that David Dempster was drowned at Granton. The dreadful story was indeed corroborated into a certainty by a bundle of clothes which the messenger of evil tidings laid on the table, no other than the suit which David had put on that morning, including the linen shirt which Dorothy's own fingers had adorned with the breast-ruffle, and identified with the beloved initials, D. D., more precious to her than the symbols of ecclesiastical honours. All were there as he had left them on the beach before the plunge which was to be unto death—yea, something after death, and more terrible, for had not David been a scoffer? If Mrs Dempster had at first been able to collect her scattered senses, she would have been satisfied even with the look of the clothes, for she had heard her husband say, with a blithe look, that he was to go to Granton to bathe, and she would, moreover, have had some minutes sooner the melancholy satisfaction that one so dear to her had not committed suicide.

But the sudden impression left no room for consolations of any kind. Struggling nature could do no more than work itself out of one swoon to fall into another, and how long it was before she could listen to the inrushing neighbours with their news that he had been boated for, and dived for, and hooked for, and searched for, no record remains to tell. But that all these efforts had been made there was no doubt, and as the hours passed bringing as yet no assuagement of a grief which is only amenable to time, it came to be known that the coast had been examined all about the fatal spot with no return but the inevitable *non inventus;* nor did it require many days to satisfy the unfortunate widow that the catastrophe was of that complete kind where the remaining victim is not only deprived of a husband, but denied the poor consolation of seeing his dead body.

Yet how true it is that the kingdom of Death is

in the land of forgetfulness, not only to the ghostly denizens who there dwell, but also to those who are left in this region of quick memories. Wherein surely there is a kindness in the cruelty; for assuredly there is no one who could suffer for a protracted period the intensity of the first onset of a grief of a privation which is to be for ever in this world and be able to live. And this kindliness of the fates was experienced by Mrs Dorothy Dempster, who, after a decent period, and amidst the consolations of friends, felt herself in a condition to be able to wait upon the creditors of her husband and get them to be contented with the small stock left by him, and give her acquittances of their debts; nay, so heartrending were her appeals, and so miserable she appeared in her weeds, that these good men even voted her a small sum out of the wreck as a beautiful tribute to pity and humanity. All which went for its value, so creditable as it is to human nature, and we need hardly add that the frequent reading of the encomium in the *Mercury* on the merits of the deceased — which, of course, proceeded on the inevitable rule that a man is only good provided he is dead—heaped up the consolation even to a species of melancholy pleasure.

And, surely, if on this occasion there was any one *ipsis charitibus humanior*, it was Mr Thomas

Snoddy, the good laird of Rubbledykes. Nor were his attentions merely empty-handed visits to the house of the widow, for he brought her money, often, after all, the chief of consolations. Of the manner in which that might be accepted he probably suspected there was nothing to be feared; but there was another gift he had in store, in regard to the acceptability of which he was not quite so sure—and that was his old love kindled up into a new flame—probably enough he had never heard or read the lines to the effect that—

> "Cupid can his wings apply,
> To other uses than to fly;
> Serving as a handkerchief
> To dry the tears of widows' grief."

But, whether so or not, he resolved upon trying what he himself could do in that remedial way; and, accordingly, he began with a small dose, the success of which urged him to a repetition; and on he went from small quantities to greater, till he was overjoyed to find that the patient could bear any amount he was able to administer. Nor could it be said that the aforesaid cough made any abatement from the success of these efforts, if we might not rather surmise that it entered as an element in their recommendation—at least it indicated no hollowness in Rubbledykes.

We all know that "the question" once meant

*torture.* At the period of our story, and we hope not less in our day, it meant *rapture;* and it is not unlikely that Mrs Dempster on that market-day, when the laird sat by the side of the parlour fire in Lady Stair's Close, enjoyed something of that kind when the words fell on her ear.

"Now, my dear Dorothy—to come to the point in the lang-run—will ye hae me for your second husband, wha should hae been your first?"

"I hae no objection," replied Dorothy, as she held away her head and covered her eyes with her handkerchief; "*but* ——"

And Mrs Dempster stopped short, with an effect almost as great on the astonished suitor as that of the memorable answer given by a certain Mrs Jean of Clavershalee to another laird, whose property lay not far distant from Rubbledykes.

"But!" ejaculated the laird, with an effort that brought an attack of his cough upon him. "You maun 'but' me nae 'buts,' Dorothy, unless ye want to kill me. I aye thought I had a better claim to you than David. Heaven rest his body in the deep waters o' the Forth, and his soul in heaven!"

"Ay," continued she, as she applied the handkerchief again, as if this time to receive some tears which ought to have come and didn't; "but that just puts me in mind o' what I was going to say.

You have seen how David was ta'en awa. What if onything should happen to you? What would become o' me? Rubbledykes would gae to your brother."

"The de'il a stane o't, Dorothy," cried the laird. "It will be a' yours. I will mak it ower to you; tofts and crofts, outhouses and inhouses, muirs and mosses, pairts and pertinents. Will that please you?"

"Ay, will 't," answered Dorothy from behind the handkerchief.

Whereupon the laird took her in his arms with a view to kiss her; but there is many a slip not only between the cup and the lip, but between one lip and another; for no sooner had Thomas so prepared himself for, perhaps, the greatest occasion of his life—even that of kissing a woman, and that woman the very idol of his heart—than that dreadful cough came again upon him, and Dorothy could not help thinking that it was now more hollow, or, as the Scotch call it, *toom*, than ever she had heard it.

"I will awa to Mr Ainslie and get the contract written out at length," he said, to cover his disgrace.

Nor was it sooner said than done. Away he went, leaving Dorothy virtually a bride, and the lady *in esse* of an estate, albeit a small one, yet great to her. At all which she laughed a most enigmatical laugh, as if some secret thoughts had risen in her mind with the effect of a ridiculous incongruity; but what these thoughts were no one ever knew. Nor shall we try to imagine them, considering ourselves to be better employed in setting forth that shortly afterwards Mrs Dorothy Dempster was joined in the silken bands of holy wedlock with Thomas Snoddy, Esquire, of Rubbledykes, and that by the hands of Dr Webster of the Tron, who accompanied the happy couple in the evening to the gray-slated mansion-house, where he made another celebration of the event by draining a couple of bottles of good old claret. Strange enough all these things; but the real wonders of our story would seem only to begin with the settlement of Mr David Dempster's widow in the mansion-house of the veritable laird; even though, consistently with the manners of the time, there was a duck-pond at the door, a peat-stack on the gable, and a midden gracing the byre not five yards from the parlour window; spite of all which Mrs Dorothy was a lady, while David lay with glazed eyes in the Forth among the fishes scarcely a mile distant from his enchanted widow.

We think it a strange thing that mortals should laugh and weep by turns, yet we think sunshine and showers a very natural alternation; and surely it is far more wonderful that we often weep when we should laugh, and laugh when we should weep —of which hypocrisy, notwithstanding, there is a hundred times more in the world than man or woman wots of. And we are sorry to be obliged to doubt the extent of the new-made lady's grief when she saw the laird's cough increasing as his love waxed stronger and his lungs grew less. Nay, we are not sure that when she saw that he was dying, and hailed the signs with grief in her eyes and joy in her heart, she was under the impression that she was acting up to the amiable tenet of her religious creed—total depravity. Be all which as it may, it is certain that though Dorothy's tears had been of that real kind of which Tully says they are—"the easiest dried of all things," they would not have retarded the progress of the laird's disease. It was not yet three months, and he was confined to bed, with Dorothy hanging over him, watching him with all the care of a seeker for favourable symptoms. But one evening there was a symptom which she was unprepared for—nay, she was this time serious in her alarm.

"I have done that which is evil in the sight o' God."

The words came as from a far-away place, they were so hollow.

"What is it, Tammas?" asked she.

"I have seen David Dempster's ghaist," said he. "It looked in at that window, and disappeared in an instant; but no' before I kent what the een said. Yea, Dorothy, they said as plainly as een can speak—'Tammas Snoddy, ye made love to Dorothy Dempster when I was alive in the body, and her lawful husband.'"

And the laird shook all over so violently that Dorothy could see the clothes move.

"Just your conscience, Tammas," said she. "Ye maun fley thae visions awa in the auld way. It is the deevil tempting ye. We maun flap the leaves o' the Bible at him, and ye'll see nae mair o' him in this warld at any rate."

And Dorothy, taking up the holy book and opening it at the middle, flapt it with such energy that more dust came out of it than should have been found in a Calvinist's Bible.

"Ye'll see nor hilt, nor hair, nor hoop, nor horn mair o' him," she added, with, we almost fear to surmise, a laugh.

And Mrs Snoddy's prophecy was of that kind— the safest of all—which comes after knowledge.

"Then I will dee in peace," said the relieved laird ; "for I hae nae ither sin on my conscience."

"Nae sin, nae salvation," added Dorothy.

"A maist comfortable doctrine," sighed the laird.

And comfortable, surely, it must have been to him, for two days afterwards the good laird slipt away out of this bad world as lightly and easily as if he had felt the burden of his sins as imponderous as the flying dove does the white feathers on its back. Nor did many more days elapse before the mortal remains of the good man were deposited in the churchyard of Cramond, leaving the double widow with her contract of marriage and her tears for a second husband lying in the earth so near the first, deep in the bosom of the Forth. But, sooner or later, there comes comfort of some kind to these amiable creatures in distress, especially if they are possessed of those cabalistic things called marriage contracts. We do not say that that comfort comes always from the grave in the shape of a veritable ghost, but sure it is that if we could in any case fancy a spirit visiting the earth for any rational purpose, it would be where a comely widow was ready to receive it, and warm its cold hands, and wrap the winding-sheet well round it, and treat it kindly. All which we may leave for suggestion and meditation, but we demand conviction, and assent, as we proceed, to set forth that the very next evening after the funeral of Laird Tammas, the ghaist of David Dempster, despising all secret openings, and even giving up the privilege of keyholes, went straight into the house of

Rubbledykes, and entered the room where Dorothy was sitting. Extraordinary enough, no doubt; but not even so much so as the fact we are about to relate—viz., that Mrs Dorothy was no more astonished at its appearance before her than she had been when she heard the laird say that he saw the face of that same spirit at the window; nor did she on this occasion have recourse to the Bible as an exorcist, by flapping the leaves of the same, to terrify it away, in the supposition that it was the devil in disguise. It is very true that she held up her hands, but then that was only a prelude to the arms being employed in clasping the appearance to her breast; an embrace which was responded to with a fervour little to be expected from one of these flimsy creatures. Nay, things waxed even more enigmatical and ridiculous, for the two actually kissed each other—a fact which ought to be treasured up as a psychological curiosity of some use, insomuch as it may diminish the fear we so irrationally feel at the expected visit of supernatural beings. But worse and more ridiculous still—

"When had you anything to eat Davie? Ye'll be hungry."

"No' unlikely, Dorothy lass," answered the wraith; "for I didna like the cauld fish, and there's nae cooking apparatus in the Forth."

"Ye would maybe tak a whang o' the round o' beef we had at the laird's funeral yesterday?"

"The very thing, woman," answered the ghaist; "and if ye have a bottle o' brandy to wash it down, it will tak awa the cauld o' the saut water."

"Twa, an ye like, lad," responded the apparently delighted widow, as she ran away to set before the visitor the edible and drinkable comforts which had been declared so acceptable.

And you may believe or reject the whisperings of our familiar just as you please, but we have all the justification of absolute veritability for the fact that this extraordinary guest, or ghaist, if you so please, sat down before the said round of beef, brandishing a knife in the one hand and a fork in the other, and looking so heartily purposed to attack the same, that you might have augured it had not had a chop since that forenoon when in the embodied state it went down to cool and wash itself in the sea at Granton. Nor need we be more squeamish than we have been in declaring at once that it did so much justice to the meat and the drink, that you might have thought it had been fed for months on Hecate's short-commons in Hades. And then a text so ample and substantial could surely bear a running commentary.

"It would have been o' nae use, Dorothy. If ye hadna been as gude a prophetess as Deborah,

I might hae been obliged to conceal myself in England lang enough."

"It didna need a Deborah, David," answered she, "to see that nae human body could stand that cough mair than a month or two. Ye hadna lang to wait, man; and though ye had had langer, *there*, see, was your comfort at the end."

And Dorothy put into the ghaist's hand the marriage contract—a worldly thing which seemed to vie with the junket of beef in its influence over mere spirit, insomuch as he perused the same by snatches between the bites and draughts, both processes going on almost simultaneously—the eye fixed on the paper, while a protruding lump in the cheek was in the act of being diminished.

"A' right, lass," was at length the exclamation.

"Ay; but ye maun be gude to me now, Davie," said she; "for ye see it's a' in my ain power: Rubbledykes is mine, and I hae wrought for 't."

"And so hae I," ejaculated the other. "You forget my banishment and difficulty of living, for I took scarcely any siller wi' me; and, mairower, how am I to face the people o' E'nbro'?"

"And the gude Calvinists o' the Tron?" added the wife.

Notwithstanding which difficulties the visitor contrived to make a hearty meal; nor was he contented with the brandy taken during the time of eating, for with all their spiritual tenderness, there was a crave for toddy — a request which was complied with by the introduction of warm water and sugar. How often the tumbler was tumbled up to pour the last drops, which defied the silver toddy-ladle in the glass, we are not authorised to say; but we have authority for the assertion that any man of flesh and blood could not have perpetrated that number of tumblings without changing almost his nature — that is, being so far spiritualised as to be entitled to say, in the words of the old song by Pinkerton —

"Death, begone — here's none but souls."

And therefore the spiritual nature of David Dempster, in his new part, was not so wonderful after all. But the doubt recurs again, as we proceed to say that Mrs Dorothy Snoddy helped her visitor to bed, nay, she actually went very blithely into that same bed herself, where they both slumbered very comfortably till next morning.

We may add that these same doubts were liable to be dispelled by another fact we have to relate. The visitor, it will be remembered, put the question to Dorothy, "How was he to meet the people of Edinburgh?" a question which implied a mortal presence, besides no prescience. We say this last deliberately, because in place of the fear of meeting being on his side, it was altogether on theirs.

It happened that, two days after the occurrences we have described, an object bearing the figure of David Dempster was seen on the Cramond road by a carrier called Samuel Finlayson, who had had transactions with the dealer in corduroys —an occasion which had the inevitable effect of raising Samuel's bonnet along with the standing hair, besides that of inducing him to whip his horse to force the animal on, just in the way of another animal of cognate species under similar circumstances. He, of course, took the story of a ghaist, all cut and dry, into the city. On the same day, Andrew Gilfillan saw the same figure on Corstorphine Hill, and flew past the seat marked "Rest and be thankful," without even looking at it. He, too, carried the same tidings. George Plenderleith encountered the identical object in the village of Corstorphine busy eating Corstorphine cream— that is, cream mixed with oatmeal, (a finer kind of crowdy,) and he hastened to Edinburgh with a speed only to be accounted for by terror. He, too, told his tale; the effect of all which, added to and inflamed by other reports, was, that Edinburgh was stirred from the Castle gate to the Palace yett, by the conviction that David Dempster had returned from the kingdom of death to this world of life for some purpose which would most certainly come out; but, in due time, whether with or without a purpose, here it was proved that ghosts were no dream, and David Hume no philosoper. Many people sought the Cramond road, and hung about Rubbledykes to get their scepticism or dogmatism confirmed. The end of these things is pretty uniform—*res locuta est;* the people began to see where the truth lay, and the laughter came in due course, to revive the hearts that had been chilled by fear.

We would be sorry if we were necessitated to end our story at the very nick of the triumph of vice. Happily, we have something more to say—nothing less, indeed, than that James Snoddy, the brother of the laird, raised a process—that is, instituted a suit before the Court of Session, to have his brother's contract of marriage with Mrs Dorothy Dempster annulled and set aside, upon the grounds of deception, circumvention, and *prava causa;* nor had he any trouble in getting a decree, for David and his wife made no appearance, neither could they make any appearance in Edinburgh. Their only resource was to take advantage of that kind of bail called "leg;" an easy affair, insomuch as there is no bond required for appearance anywhere. It was at the time supposed that they had gone to America, that asylum of unfortunates, where one half of the people cut the throats of the other in the name of liberty.

## The Story of the Gorthley Twins.

IT was the custom at one time in Edinburgh for the proprietors of large self-contained houses to give them the names of the properties they had in the country—hence our Panmure House, Tweeddale Court, and so forth—and among them there was Gorthley House, of which no vestige now remains; nay, we are by no means sure where it was situated, beyond the fact that it was somewhere in the Canongate, but gone as it is according to the law of change, its name will always be associated with the law-plea Bruce *versus* Bruce, which contained the germ of the little romance we are now to relate in our way. And to begin in order, we take the state of matters at the time when the plea began. John Bruce of Gorthley had died, and left a widow and three daughters, two of whom were twins, and the third was the youngest. The names of the twins were Sarah and Martha, who at this time were two fine girls verging upon majority, and as like each other as two white peas; and surely if we might expect, in this world of strife and contention, that there should be found real love and friendship anywhere, it might be in the case of two sisters who had lain so close together for nine months, and who had drunk their milk at the same kindly fountain of a doating mother's breast. But so full is the moral atmosphere of our fallen world of the spores of hatred, that you may as well try to keep a cheese from the seeds of green mould as the human heart from the germs of ill-will. And so it was that these two young ladies hated each other very heartily, for a reason which we will by and by reveal, to the astonishment of the reader; and this hatred was the counterpart of a contention that had embittered the lives of the father and mother, even up to the time of the former's death.

All which will be better explained by following the course of events after the death of Mr Bruce, beginning with a visit on the part of Lady Gorthley —as she was called according to the custom of the time, when titles were held in such regard that the common people even forged them for the great— along with her favourite daughter, Martha, to the office of Mr James Pollock, the agent for the family. That her ladyship was bent upon some enterprise of considerable moment might have been guessed from the look of her face, which had that mysterious air about it belonging to secrecy, nor less from that of the daughter; and no one could have doubted that, whatever they were bent upon, the other twin, Sarah, was not to be let up to the secret. Perhaps the time of the visit to the writer was opportune, insomuch as Sarah had gone, as she had said, with her cousin, George Walkinshaw, advocate, to take a stroll by the back of St Leonard's as far as "the Cat Nick," and come home by the Hunter's Bog; which couple, we may also say, had their secret too, in addition to their love affair, if that secret was not connected with the very same subject we have referred to as that which divided the family. Be all that as it might, we are going right along with the facts of the plea when we set forth that in a very short time Lady Gorthley and Martha were seated each on a chair in the writing office of the said agent, Mr Pollock, and the very first words that came out of her ladyship's mouth were these—

"Has Sarah or her cousin called upon you since the death of Gorthley?" by which she meant, according to the custom of the time, her own husband.

"They are even at this moment in the other room, madam," said he, with a lawyer's smile on his face.

"Indeed," said her ladyship, with an expression

of both surprise and anger. "Why, she told me an hour ago that she was going to take a walk by the 'Cat Nick.'"

"And so she has," added the writer, still smiling, "for my door may not be inappropriately so called in the circumstances?"

"Only, I presume," said the lady, "I am not, I hope, to be included among the cats. I will wait until you have learned what the impertinent girl has got to say, and then you will have time to hear me and Martha."

"I already know that," said he; "but, as I believe our conversation is about finished, I will despatch them in a few seconds, and then return to hear your ladyship's commands."

"But you will say nothing of our being here."

"The never a word, madam," said he, adding to himself as he went away, "I don't want a battle of the cats in my office at least; they do best when they put the cheese into the hands of the ———," and he did not add the word monkey, insomuch as it looked personal.

"There, you see, Martha, the gipsy is determined to stand by her rights," was the remark of her ladyship after Mr Pollock had left the room.

"But we'll beat her off, mother," rejoined Martha, with a spirit which Mr Pollock or any other lawyer might have admired; "and," continued Martha, with a smile, "we will say nothing about the *strawberry*."

"Nothing, dear," rejoined the mother; "that strawberry is worth all the lands of Gorthley."

Of which enigmatical strawberry they said no more; but that is no reason why we should not say something of it when the proper time comes, of which, by the rules of our art, we are the best judges. Meanwhile Mr Pollock, having despatched the other feline, returned.

"And now, madam," said he, as he took his seat, "I am ready to hear you."

"You know, Mr Pollock," resumed her ladyship, "that the entail of Gorthley provides that the property shall go to the eldest heir female in the event of there being no heir male."

"We all know that, madam," said the writer; "and if we had any doubt of it a certain paper in that green box there would very soon clear up our vision. But the question is, which of the two young ladies, Sarah or Martha, first saw the light of day?"

"No question at all," rejoined the lady. "Martha was the first born."

"Yes, madam, I know, and knew before, that that is your opinion; but you are perhaps not aware that Gorthley himself told me, some time before he died, that Sarah was the first born; and so we have here, so far as the testimony goes, one witness against another."

"And what knew he about it?" retorted she, sharply. "He was not present at the birth to see; while I fancy you won't deny I was."

Whereupon Mr Pollock, getting into the mistake that her ladyship was drolling, and being a droll himself, said, laughing, "Why, madam, no man could deny the necessity of your being present any more than in the case of Girzel Jamphrey, who said to the people who were pressing on to see her burnt as a witch on the sands at Dundee, 'You needna be in sic a hurry; there will be nae sport till I come.'"

Whereat Lady Gorthley tightened the strings she had allowed to get loose.

"It's not a matter to joke about, sir," she said. "Though I am not a witch, I say, and will maintain, that I am a better witness to the fact of which of the twins was born first than Gorthley could possibly be."

"Still, madam," continued the writer, "I fear it is only a comparison between the value of two ciphers; the one may look bigger than the other, but each is equal to nothing. It is true that we men don't know much of these things, yet—I beg pardon, the subject is a little delicate—we know that when a lady bears twins she doesn't take the first and mark it before she bears the second; and then if she doesn't mark it in the very nick of time, it's of no use, because the two babies get mixed in the bath, as an Irishman would say, and their being so like as one strawberry to another, no one can say that the one is not the other, or the other not the one."

At which mention of the word strawberry, Lady Gorthley looked to Martha, and Martha looked to her, and they seemed puzzled.

"But however all that may be," continued the lady, "what can you say to the evidence of Peggy Macintosh, the nurse, who will swear that Martha came first into the world?"

"I cannot answer that question," said he, with the caution of his profession, "until I see Mrs Macintosh and examine her. There is also Jean Gilchrist, one of the servants, who was present, I have her to examine also, and then we will see where the truth lies. Oh! but I forgot there is Mrs Glennie, the midwife, the woman whose word will go farthest, because she had a better *causa scientiæ.*"

"I know nothing about Latin," rejoined her ladyship angrily; "but as for Mrs Glennie, she's dead years ago."

"Ah, indeed," said Mr Pollock, "if that is true we will have only the nurse and the servant for witnesses, and if they oppose each other, the one for Sarah and the other for Martha, and as it is true that you always treated Martha as the eldest, and Gorthley always insisted on Sarah as being the first-born, we will have an undecidable case, a thing that never occurred in Scotland before, perhaps not in the world, for you know Solomon would not allow any impossibility in deciding the case of the baby with the two mothers. But, madam, allow me to say, that as your husband, Mr Bruce, left directions that I, as agent for the family, should get Sarah served heir, and as you insist upon that being done for Martha, it will be necessary that you employ a man of business of your own, so that we may fight the battle fair out."

"Well," said the lady with an expression of bitterness in her face not much in harmony with her words, "since Gorthley has left the continuance of the strife as a legacy to his widow and children, I shall go to Mr Bayne as my agent, and authorise him to protect the rights of Martha, and fight it to the bitter end—bitter, I mean, for Sarah Bruce, who will never be Lady Gorthley."

And with these words she left, accompanied by Martha, directing their steps to the office of Mr Bayne, who, as her ladyship's private agent, knew very well of this most strange contention which had so long been maintained in Gorthley House.

Nor, probably, was he displeased at it, any more than Mr Pollock had been. Gorthley estate was a large cheese, the cats were fierce, and there was plenty for even two monkeys, so he listened attentively to her ladyship's statement that the nurse, Mrs Macintosh, would swear in favour of Martha, but she said never a word about Jean Gilchrist.

"The nurse's evidence will go a great way, madam," said he, "seeing the midwife is dead; but it will be satisfactory if Mrs Macintosh could condescend upon some mark which she noticed immediately at the time of the birth, for the two young ladies are really so like each other now I often confound them, nay, they confound me so that we cannot very well imagine how they could be distinguished when brought together soon after birth."

"Look here, Mr Bayne," said the lady in a whispering way, as if she were to reveal something wonderously mysterious, "look here, sir,"—

And taking off Martha's cloak and turning up the kerchief that covered her neck and the top of her shoulders, she said, "Do you see that?"

The writer complied by a pretty narrow inspection of a very pretty neck of (a strawberry being in question) the appropriate colour of cream.

"A very decided mark of a strawberry," said he; "and, really if it were a proof that Martha has the right to succeed to Gorthley, it might be said to be the most beautiful beauty spot that a young lady could bear. How comes that mark to be there?"

"Why," replied the lady, "Gorthley threw a strawberry at me when I was in the way, you know, and thus made a mother's mark, as they call it, just as if he had intended to point out the true heir; and you know the Scotch say that these marks are lucky."

"But you forget, madam," replied the man of the law, who did not believe in special providences, except in special cases, when he received payment of his accounts. "You forget that Gorthley was against Martha, so that if he had had any intention in the matter, it must rather have been to make a blot; besides, our judges might probably say that the mark, for aught they knew, was intended to show that Martha was not the heir; in short, unless we can identify the mark as having been seen on the first-born, I fear, though it is very pretty, it will do us no good."

"But Mrs Macintosh can do that," replied the lady.

"Ah! you have hit the mark now," said he; "and I will see Mrs Macintosh, and any other witnesses who can speak to the point."

And so having, after some more conversation, despatched his two clients, Mr Bayne procceded that same evening to the residence of Mrs Peggy

Macintosh, whom he found very busy spinning, little prepared for a visit from a man of the law, with a powdered wig on his head, and a gold-headed cane in his hand,—an apparition which even the wheel could not resist, for it stopt its birr instantly, as if through fear.

"Mrs Macintosh," said Mr Bayne, as he took a seat alongside of Peggy, "do you remember having been present at the birth of Mrs Bruce's twins?"

"Indeed, sir, and I was," answered she, "and a gey birth it was."

"And could you tell which was which when the infants were born?"

"Weel, sir," answered Peggy, "if you will tell me which is the which you mean, I'll try to satisfy ye if I can?"

"Why, I mean, which was Sarah and which Martha?" continued the writer.

"How could I tell ye that, sir," answered Peggy, with a look of true Scotch complacency, "when the bairns werena christened?"

The writer, acute as he was, was a little put out, but he rallied.

"Why, Peggy, you surely understand what I mean; did you not know the child which was afterwards called Sarah from that which was afterwards called Martha?"

"I would have liked to have seen you try that, sir," was again the answer. "How the deil—I beg pardon, sir—was I to ken what they were to be ca'ed when their names werena even fixed by the father and mother themselves?"

"I see you don't understand me, Mrs Macintosh," continued Mr Bayne, who had got a Scotch witness on his line.

"I think it's you that doesna understand me," retorted Peggy.

"Look here," continued Mr Bayne, smiling, "you know Sarah Bruce and Martha Bruce?"

"Ay, when they're thegither," replied Peggy, "and they tell me their names; but just put them an ell or twa asinder, and I'll defy the horned Clootie himsel to say which is which."

"Worse and worse," muttered the writer. "Look you, Peggy, was there no mark on either of the children by which you could know it?"

"Ay was there," replied the woman; "but we're just where we were; for, whether the strawberry was upon the ane or the ither, or the ither or the ane, is just what I want you, since you're a man o' the law, and weel skilled in kittle points, to tell me."

"Worse even yet," muttered the discomfited precognoscer.

"But I can mak the thing as plain as the Shorter

Catechism," continued she, with a sharp look, which revived the sinking hopes of Mr Bayne. "Mrs Glennie that night was in a terrible fluster, for she began to see that there was likely to be mair bairns than she bargained for—twins, if no may be trins ; so Jean Gilchrist was brought up to help in addition to mysel. Then the first ane cam' in a hurry, the mair by token it kenned naething o' the warld it was coming into, and Mrs Glennie pushed it into my hands. 'There will be anither, Peggy,' said she, 'and look gleg ;' but there was only flannel for ane ; and I gave the wean to Jean to wash, while I ran to get happins. I was back in less than five minutes ; and, just as I was entering, 'Here's the other ane,' said Mrs Glennie. I took it frae her, and gave it to Jean, and took frae her the ane she had washed, in order to wrap it, and so I did ; but before I was dune I saw Jean wasna doing the thing as she ought ; so I gave her the ane I had, and I took hers to wash it better ; but before it was dune Mrs Glennie cried to me to come to help her with the lady ; so I put my bairn into Jean's arms alang side o' the ither ; and when I had finished with the lady I took the last ane frae Jean again ; but before I had completed the dressing o't Jean cried out, 'This bairn is decin'.' 'You're a fule,' said I, 'give it to me ;' and so she did. Then I ran and got some cordial, and poured it down the throat o' the creature. By this time Jean had hers upon the settee, and I laid mine alang side o't; but in a little time the mither was crying to see the weans; and Mrs Glennie took the ane, and I took the ither, and showed her them. Then Mrs Glennie took mine away to lay it down on the settee again; and I took hers and laid it down by the side o' its sister. That's how it was, sir, and sure I am naething can be plainer."

"But what about the strawberry?" said Mr Bayne.

"Nane o' us saw that till the bairns began to be mixed," was the answer; "and then they were changed, and changed again sae aften that my head ran round, and I lost a' count."

"But haven't you said to Lady Gorthley that the mark was on the first-born?" asked Mr Bayne.

"Indeed, and I did that same," was the ready answer. "My lady gave me five gowden guineas to tell her; and, as I couldna be sure, I thought I couldna do better than to make safe and sure wark o't; so I took five shillings out o' the five guineas and gave it to the Carlin o' the Cowgate, a wise woman, frae the very native place o' thae far-seeing creatures, Auldearn, Auld Eppie, as they ca' her, (they were all Eppies,) and she settled the thing in the trice o' a cantrup; so you see the fact is sure that the strawberry belanged to the first-born."

"And did you tell Lady Gorthley you went to Eppie?" inquired the discomfited writer.

"Gude faith na, she might hae asked back the five guineas," answered Peggy; "and besides, if she got the truth, it was a' ane to her, ye ken, where it cam' frae; and you'll be discreet and say naething."

"Did you ask from the old woman the name of her who bore the mark?" rejoined Mr Bayne.

"Ay, but she said she didna like to spier that at the auld ane—Nick, ye ken—because he might have got angry and told her a lee, and that might hae brought me into a scrape wi' her ladyship, who knew hersel which o' her daughters bore the mark."

"Very prudent," muttered again the writer, as he rose, "this is a most satisfactory witness."

And carrying this satisfaction along with him, he proceeded to the small garret occupied by Jean Gilchrist, the direction to which he had got from Mrs Macintosh. Believing as he did the statement made to him by the latter, he had very little hope of getting anything satisfactory out of his present witness, and wishing to keep her more to the point than he had been able to effect in the prior case, he assumed her presence at the birth, and came straight out with the question, whether she knew if there had been noticed on one of the children the mark of the strawberry.

"The strawberry?" said she, "ay, wi' a' wondered at that, but then it's no uncommon things in weans to be marked in that way, so we sune got ower 't."

"And was this mark on the child which was first born?" inquired he.

"I'll tell you that, sir," replied she, "if ye'll tell me first which o' the twa cam' first into the world."

Whereby Mr Bayne found himself where he was, in the hands of a Scotch metaphysician, for, was there not here an example of the *à priori* argument, to use the old jargon, wherein the cause is assumed to prove the effect, and the effect is then brought forward to prove the cause—a trick of wisdom we are yet in the nineteenth century playing every day?

"That is just what I want to know, Jean," said he.

"And it's just what I want to ken, too," rejoined Jean, "for to tell you God's truth, sir," she continued in a lower tone, "I hae something on my conscience, and yet it's no muckle either."

"And what is that?" said he, expecting to get at something on which he could rely, whatever it might be.

"Just this," answered Jean. "Years agane, Gorthley came to me, and said, 'Jean Gilchrist, here is something for you,' and I took it—it was a purse o' gowd,—and then he said, 'I would die happy, Jean, if I could think that Martha Bruce, who bears the mark, was the second born of my daughters;' and, looking at the purse, said I, 'Weel, sir, if that will mak ye happy, ye may be happy, for it was even so.' Then said he, 'Will you stand to that, Jean?' And I said, 'Ay, will I, through thick and thin;' and when he went away, I began to consider if I had dune wrang, but I couldna see it, for doesna the Bible say, that man and wife are ane flesh? and if that be true, how could their children be separate flesh? Weel then, whichever o' the twa, the first or the second born, carried the mark, they baith being ane flesh, behoved to bear it, and so, if the ane bore it the other bore it, and if the other bore it the ane bore it. Besides, wha doesna ken that twins are just ae bairn cut in twa? They're aye less than the single bairns, and isna a double-yokit egg just twa eggs joined thegither into ane."

A kind of logic common at the time, and which, indeed, touched upon the most obscure question of metaphysics, and not very satisfactory to Mr Bayne, who, however, knew the subtle character of the Scotch mind too well to try a fall with so acute a dialectician. So, altogether disappointed with his precognition he left and came away, meeting in the passage Mr Pollock, who had been with Mrs Macintosh, and was now on his way to Jean Gilchrist. They were very intimate, and did not hesitate to compare notes, the result of which was that the case was to realise once more the truth of the toast generally drunk by Edinburgh practitioners at the end of the session, " The glorious uncertainty;" and if Mr Pollock thought so before he examined Jean Gilchrist, his opinion must have been pretty well confirmed by what she said. The case, in short, was not one in which there is conflicting evidence, and where the judges can make out the weight by a hair of prejudice; it was a case in which there was no evidence at all as to which of the girls was the heir; but, then, it was just on account of this equipoise that the two claimants, Martha, helped by her mother on the one side, and Sarah, supported by her lover, Walkinshaw, on the other, waxed the more bitter; and the contention which had so long raged in Gorthley House became hotter and hotter. Nor need we fancy that the writers would try to get the right compromised in some way, where they had so good a chance of making a money certainty out of a moral uncertainty; and so the case went into court under two competing briefs, that is just two claims by the daughters, each insisting to be served heir. The witnesses, whose precognitions we have given, were examined; and a great number of servants who had been in the family, who swore that Gorthley himself always called Sarah Miss Bruce, and Mrs Bruce always called Martha by that dignified title, so that the servants tried to please both master and mistress by calling the one daughter or the other miss, just according to the chance of being overheard by the heads of the house. When before the sheriff, and when the claims were equally suspended, a strange plea was set up by Sarah's counsel, Mr Fotheringham, to the effect that, taking the question of priority of birth to be doubtful, the doubt could be resolved by a kind of *nobile officium* on the part of the father as the head of the house, and that as Gorthley had declared for Sarah this should be held as sufficient; but Mr Maitland answered this by saying that the question being one of fact, and that fact coming more within the presumed knowledge of the mother, ought to be settled by the voice of the mother, who declared for Martha; and here again the argument being nearly equal, the judge on the inquest was nonplussed. And thus it came to pass that the old irony of the ancients, directed against a sow coming in place of Minerva as a judge of some very fine matter of truth, turned out to be in this case no irony at all, for the sow was here as good a judge as Minerva. The scales were so nearly balanced that the mere breath which conveyed the doubt might disperse the doubt by moving one of the scales—a very fine irony in itself, in so much as all truth may be resolved, in the far end, into the mere breath of man's opinion. At length the sheriff gave the cast of the scale to the side of the mother, as the "*domestic witness.*"

But Saraḥ was, of course, dissatisfied; or, rather, Fotheringham, who advised her to take the case before the Fifteen, by what is called an Advocation, and so to be sure these lords got a burden thrown upon them which cost them no little trouble. They got the case argued and argued, and were in the end so mystified, that if they could have decided that the question was undecidable, they would have been very glad to have hung it up among the eternal dubieties as an everlasting proof of "the glorious uncertainty;" but they could not agree even to do that, for the entail could not be compromised or set aside, and so they behoved to decide one way or another. Meanwhile, the case having made a noise, a great number of people were collected in court on the day when the judgment was to be finally given. And given it was so far, for seven judges were for Sarah, and seven for Martha, so it came to the president, who said,

"I have read of a case somewhere in which the judges drew cuts, and decided by the Goddess Chance in place of justice; and, indeed, if the latter is blind, as they say she is, we may take the one as well as the other as the umpire of the right or the wrong. But there is one consideration which moves me in this case, and that is, that as it is the wife's duty to bear the children of the family, so it is her privilege to know more about that interesting affair than the husband, who is, as I understand, never present at the mysteries of Lucina, and, therefore, I would be inclined to declare that Martha was the first-born."

"It's a lee, my lord," cried a shrill screaming voice from the court. Whereat the judges directed their eyes with much amazement to the place whence the scream came.

"And who are you," said the president, "who dare to speak in a court of justice?"

"I deny it's a court o' justice," cried the voice again. "My name is Janet Glennie, and it was me that had the first handlin' o' the bairns, and I tell your lordship to your face, that you're clean wrang, and ken nae mair about the case than Jenkins did about the colour o' the great grandmother o' his hen. I tell ye it was Sarah wha came first, and Martha wi' her strawberry came second, for I saw the mark wi' my ain een."

A speech followed by the inevitable laugh of a curious audience, and the better received that the people had always a satirical feeling against the fifteen wise wigs. Nor was this late testimony too late: Mrs Glennie was subsequently sworn, and the judgment went for Sarah. It turned out that Mrs Glennie had been absent for a time from Scotland, and, having, upon visiting Edinburgh, heard of the famous trial, made it a point to be present. Nay, there was a little retribution in the affair, for Lady Gorthley knew she was alive, and had reported her death to serve her own ends.

## The Story of the Chalk Line.

FOR the truth of the story I am now to relate I have the word of a godly minister of the Church of Scotland, whose father had been in the house in Burnet's Close, and had seen the two females and examined "the chalk line" in the middle of the floor. I do not say this to conciliate your belief; for perhaps if this were my object, I should be nearer the attainment of it by asserting, as Mr Thackeray used to do when he wanted his readers to believe him, that there is not a word of truth in the whole affair. There is a certain species of fish in the Ganges which is never happy but when it is pushing up against the stream; and people, as civilisation goes on, find themselves so often cheated, that they go by contraries, just as the old sorcerers divined by reading backwards. But surely in this age of subtleties it is a pleasant thing to think that you are so much the object of an author's care as that he would not only save you from thinking, but think for you; and so I proceed to tell you of the personages in Burnet's Close, leading from the High Street to the Cowgate.

In a room of the second flat of the third tall tenement on your left hand as you descend lived Martha and Mary Jopp. They were, so far as I have been able to discover, the daughters of a writer of the name of Peter Jopp. You cannot be wrong in supposing that they had been once young, though, in regard to the aged, this is not always conceded by those who are buoyant with the spirit of youth. Yes, these aged maidens had not only been once young, they had been very fair and very comely. They had passed through the spring and summer flowers without treading upon the speckled serpent of the same colour. They had heard the song of love where there was no risk of the deceptions of the siren. They had been tempted; but they had resisted the temptation of some who could well have returned their affection. Nor was this the result of any want of natural sensibility; if it was not that they had too much of that quality, which, if it is the source of pleasure, is also that of pain—perhaps more of the latter than the former, though we dare not say so in this our time of angelic perfection.

To be a little more particular upon a peculiarity

of our two ladies, which enters as rather a "loud colour" in the web of our story, there was a sufficient reason for their celibacy. They had a mother who, as the saying goes, was "a woman of price"—such a one as Solomon excepts from so many, that I am afraid to mention the number. She was a good Calvinist, without insisting too much for election and predestination. She was affectionate, without the weakness which so often belongs to doating mothers; and she possessed, along with the charm of universal kindness, a strength of mind which demanded respect without diminishing love. No wonder that her daughters loved her even to that extent that neither of the two could think of leaving her so long as she lived. An inclination this, or rather a resolution, which had been confirmed in them by certain experiences they had had of what their mother had suffered from having been deprived by death of an elder daughter, and by marriage of a younger; the latter of whom had gone with her husband, a Mr Darling, to Calcutta, under the patronage of Major Scott, the friend of Warren Hastings.

But there was another reason which kept the sisters from marrying—one which will, I suspect, be very slow to be believed; and that was, their love for each other. But I am resolute in urging it, because, in the first place, it is not absolutely against the experience of mankind ; and, secondly, because, while it forms a part of the story as narrated to me, it is necessary as one of the two sides of a contrast, without which I could not answer for a certain effect in my picture. Certain, at least, it was that more than one external revolving body in the shape of lovers came within the sphere of their attraction for each other, and could produce no deflection in the lines of their mutual attachment. It was said that one of them had been jilted. I do not know; but the circumstance would explain a fact more certain that the sisters, in their then lively humour of young blood, used to sing a love-defiance song, which might have been both sport and earnest. My informant gave me the words. It is a kind of rough mosaic, with borrowed verses, yet worth recording :—

> A farmer's daughter fair am I,
>    As blithe as May-day morning,
> And when my lover passes by,
>    I laugh at him wi' scorning.
>       Ha! ha! ha! fal lal la!
>       Ha! ha! fal lal laldy!
>
> There came a cock to our father's flock,
>    And he wore a double kaim, O ;
> He flapt his wings, and fain would craw,
>    But craw he could craw nane, O.
>
> A braw young man came courting me,
>    And swore his wife he'd make me ;
> But when he knew my pounds were few,
>    The rogue he did forsake me.

> Gae whistle on your thumb, young man,
>   You left me wae and weary;
> But, now I've got my heart again,
>   Gude faith, I'll keep it cheery.
>
> There's world's room for you to pass,
>   And room enough for Nan, O;
> The deil may tak her on his back
>   Who dies for faithless man, O.
>
> There's still as good fish in the sea
>   As ever yet were taken;
> I'll spread my net and catch again,
>   Though I have been forsaken.
>     Ha! ha! ha! &c.

A better medicine, I suspect, than an action of damages. But to continue. The sisters read the same books, took the same walks, wrought at the same work as steadfastly and lovingly as they worshipped the same mother, and revered the memory of the same father—a remark this last which helps us on to a point of our story; for the father had been dead for some years, leaving the mother a competent annuity, besides a residue, which would afford at least so much to the daughters as would tocher them to a kind of independence, though not to a husband with much hope of being benefited in a money point of view by marriage. But the time came—as what time does not come, even to those who think in the heyday of their happiness it will never come—when there would be a change, when the charm of this threefold relation should cease.

The mother died, and with her the annuity; and the attraction she had exercised over the daughters had just drawn them so far past the point of the shaking of the blossoms of youth and beauty and hope, that their affection for each other stood now no chance of being broken by even one of those moral comets that burn up more incombustible bodies than old spinsters with very small competences.

And so, with bleared eyes of uncontrollable grief, and no hope, and a trifle of twenty pounds a-year each to be paid them by Mr David Ross, writer, their father's agent, our two spinsters took up their solitary residence in the foresaid room in the second flat of the big tenement in Burnet's Close to which I have alluded. Even at the first moment of their retreat they seem to have shaken off with the blossoms, which, in the human plant no less than in the vegetable one, alone contain the beauties and sweets of life—the stem being, alas, only at best the custodier of an acid—much of their interest in the busy, gossipping, scandalising, hating, and loving Edinburgh; but so far this resistance to the charms of the outer world only served to make them live even more and more to each other. And then, had they not the sweet though melancholy solace of that Calvinistic tenet which imparted such mildness and equanimity to the face of their beloved mother—even that mysterious scroll which contains the ordination and predestination of all things which shall ever come to pass? Yes; but even this solace was modified by the regret that the portrait of that mother, painted by no unskilful hand—a pupil of George Jameson's—was not, as it ought to have been, in that room hanging over the mantelpiece; the more by reason that that picture had been surreptitiously taken away by their sister Margaret when she sailed with her husband, Mr Darling, to India. And would they not have it back? Mr Ross might tell them when he was there on a certain evening.

"You have as good a right to it," said the man of the law, "as your sister; for I believe it was never given to her by your mother."

"No more it ever was," said Martha; "for did not our mother write herself for it, but it never came; and she was to have got herself painted again, but death came at the predestinated hour, and took away her life, and with it all our happiness in this world."

"Not all your happiness, Miss Martha," rejoined the agent; "for have you not your mutual affection left?—ay, and even your love for her who is only removed to a distance—even among blessed spirits?—from whence she is at this moment looking down upon you to bless that love which you

U

bear to each other, and which, I trust, will never decay."

"I hope not," said Mary, calmly; "but I remember how, when the evil spirit took hold of us, and made us fretful and discontented with each other, she calmed our rebellious spirits by a look so justly reproving, and yet so mild and heavenly-like, that for very love of her we would dote on each other the more. And now I think if we had that picture, with the same eye as if still fixed on us, we would be secured against all fretfulness; for O sir, we are all weak and wilful. Will you write for it, Mr Ross? It would hang so well up there over the fire, where, you see, there is an old nail, which seems to have been left by the former tenant for the very purpose."

"I will," replied Mr Ross; "but I may as well tell you I have little chance of success, for Margaret, I suspect, would nearly as soon part with her life. Nor do I wonder at it; for the countenance of your mother as there represented seems so far above that of ordinary mortals, both in beauty and benignity, that methinks,"—and here Mr Ross smiled in his own grave way,—"if I ever felt inclined to put down six-and-eightpence against a client in place of three-and-fourpence, that look of hers would bring back my sense of honesty. You know I have Mrs Ross over the mantelpiece of my business room; and though she never approached your mother in that peculiar expression, which your father used to say to me, in a half-jocular way, humanised him into that wonderful being, a conscientious writer, yet I have been benefited in the same way by the mild light of my Agnes's eyes."

And Mr Ross stopped, in consequence of feeling a small tendency to a thickening in the throat, which he seldom felt except when he had a cold.

"And you will write Margaret, then?" resumed Martha.

"That I will," said he; "but I do not say may Heaven bless my effort, because you know Heaven has made up its mind on that and all other subjects long ago."

"Even from the foundations of the earth," sighed Mary.

"Even so," rejoined Mr Ross as he departed, leaving the sisters to their small supper of a Newhaven haddock, each half of which was sweetened to the receiver by the consciousness that the other was being partaken of by her sister. And thereafter, having said their prayers, they retired to the same bed, to fall asleep in each other's arms, without a regret that said arms were not a little more sinewy, or that their faces did not wear beards, and to dream of their mother.

And it would have been well if affairs in Burnet's Close had continued to go on as smoothly as we have here indicated. Nor did there seem any reason why they should not. The sisters had a sufficiency to live on; they had no evil passions to disturb the equanimity of their thoughts; they were religious, and resigned to the predestinated; they were among "the elect," that is, orthodoxically, they elected to think so, which is the same thing. They had their house in order, and could afford to have Peggy Fergusson to clean out the room occasionally, and to go the few messages that their few wants required. But Time is a sower as well as a reaper; and he casts about with an equally ready hand the seeds of opinions and imaginations, the germs of feelings and the spores of mildewed hopes: some for the young, some for the old, but all inferring change from what was yesterday to what is to-day; from what is to-day to what will be to-morrow. As the days passed into years, they appeared to get shorter and shorter—a process with all of us, which no theory can explain, if it is not against all theory; for if time is generated by ideas, it should appear to go more slowly the more slowly those ideas arise and pass, and yet the practical effect of the working is the very reverse. But whatever were the changes that were taking place in the habits and feelings of the two sisters, they were altogether unconscious of them. The indisposition to go out and mix with their friends was gradually increasing, as they felt, without being aware of the feeling, that they had less and less in common with the ways of the world; and the seldomer they went out, the seldomer their friends came to see them, nor when they did come, did they receive any encouragement to repeat the visit.

In all this I do not consider that I am describing human nature in the aspect in which we generally see it; for we more often find in those who are advancing into age a felt necessity for enlivenment, were it for nothing else than to relieve them from solitary musings and the perilous stuff of old memories; but here, as it will by and by be seen, I have not to do with ordinary human nature. These sisters were fated to be strange, and to do strange things. The indisposition to go out degenerated in the course of some years into a love of total seclusion. They never passed the threshold of their room; and as time went on, their friends gradually renounced their efforts to get either of them to change a purpose to which they seemed to have attained by the sympathy of two natures exactly similar. They probably knew nothing of the words of the poet, nor would they have cared for them:—

> "The world careth not a whit
> For him who careth not for it:
> One only duty and one right,
> That he be buried out of sight."

But amidst this strange asceticism the one still remained to the other as a dear, loving, and beloved sister; and if all the world should be nothing to them, they would still be all the world to each other. The seclusion had lasted five years since the death of the mother, and still no decay of their mutual attachment could be observed.

It is here that commences the wonderful part of my story,—so wonderful, indeed, that if I had not had at second-hand the testimony of an eye-witness, confirmed by the traditions of the Close, I could scarcely have ventured the recital I here offer; not that I consider the facts as unnatural, but that the causes which change love into hatred, and superinduce the latter often in a direct ratio to the former, lie so deep, and are altogether so mysterious, that we cannot understand the meaning of their being there, and far less how they came to be there. Some strange and unaccountable change came over these hitherto loving sisters, not only at the same time, but without its having ever been ascertained that there was any physical or moral reason for it. It began to show itself in small catches and sharper rejoinders; minim points not discernible by their former love became subjects of difference. Then the number of these increased where the points of contact were, as one might say, infinite. They assert that nature resents too close an affinity of affection; nor is this altogether theory, for we see every day friendships which are so close as to merge identities flare up into terrible hatreds; and we have scriptural authority for the wrath of brothers. A plain man would get out of the difficulty in a plain way. Those sisters had become discontented because they had rejected that natural food of the mind which is derived from an intercourse with the world; and who does not know that discontent always finds a peg somewhere whereon to hang a grievance. Where you have many people about you, you have a greater choice of these pegs; if you are cooped up in a room with only one human being within your vision, you are limited; but the pegs must be got, and *are* got, till the whole of the one object, a miserable scapegoat, is covered with them.

Probably the plain man is right. I leave him to the philosopher, and keep to my safe duty as a narrator.

The spirit of fault-finding once begun, waxed stronger and stronger upon the food it generated by its own powers of production. Almost everything either of them did appeared to be wrong in the eyes of the other; and though for a time they tried to repress the sharp feelings, which were wonders even to themselves, yet the check would come, the taunt would follow, and the flash of the eye—an organ once so expressive of love—succeeded within the passing minute. People who merely meet may be supposed to seek for objects of disagreement. In the room in Burnet's Close the occasions were the very actions of natural life; the movements of the body, the words of the mouth, the glances of the eye, the thoughts of the mind, the misconstrued feelings of the heart. Nor could they, as in most cases people who disagree may, get away from each other. The repulsion which they felt towards a world which offered them only reminiscences of past joys, was as a wall enclosing the arena where these gladiatorial displays of feeling went on from day to day, scarcely even interrupted by the holy Sabbath any more than if they had come within the excepted category of necessity and mercy.

According to my information, which descended to the minutest particulars, this domestic disease went on for years, without any other alteration than changes consistent with the laws of bodily ailment. There were exasperations which, expending themselves in gratuitous vituperations, receded into silent sullennesses, which lasted for days. If it happened that no grievance could be discovered by the microscopic vision, there was recourse to the grievance of yesterday, which was called up to occupy the greedy vacuum; and then the changes of aspect, of which, to the jaundiced eye, it was capable, were rung upon it till they were physically wearied of the strife: while the weariness only lasted till a renewed energy became ripe for another onset. But however high the exasperation ever reached, they never came to any violence. All the energy expended lay in the tongue, and the eye, and the contorted muscles of irrascible expression. It might have been doubted whether, if any third party interfered, the one would not have defended the other; but only to retain her as valuable property for the onset of her peculiar privilege. And what is not less strange, their religion, which was still maintained with the old Calvinistic dogmatism, in place of overcoming the domestic demon, became subjected to it, and changed its aspect according to the wish. Though incapable of inflicting any bodily pain upon each other, they felt no compunction in fostering the opinion that, while each was among the elect and predestinated to everlasting glory, the other was in the scroll of the reprobate, and ordained to eternal punishment in the brimstone fires, and the howling horrors of the pit which is so peculiarly constituted as to have no bottom. Each would read her Bible in her own chair, and shoot against the other glances of triumph as she figured herself in heaven looking down upon the torments of her sister in hell. And all this while neither could have with her own hands inflicted the scratch of a pin upon the body of the other. It was enough that each could lacerate the feelings of the other as a vent to the exasperation which embittered her own heart.

Still more remarkable, there were none of these reconciliations that among relations often make amends for strife, and maintain the equipoise so insisted upon by nature. We all know how these ameliorations work in the married life and among lovers. In these cases the anger seems to become the fuel of love. Not so with our sisters. The worm was a never-dying one. But even in this desperate case there was not wanting evidence of nature's efforts towards an amelioration. It was true they could not separate; they were objects necessary to each other; nay, even if Mr Ross, who witnessed the working of the domestic evil, had contrived to get them into separate rooms—a proposal which was indeed made, and morbidly resisted—they would have pursued each other in imagination with perhaps even more misery than that which they inflicted on each other.

At length they came to a scheme of their own, so peculiar that it has formed the incident of that story which has made it live in Edinburgh through many years, and even to this day. The plan was, that they should draw in the middle of the floor a distinct line of chalk, which should be a boundary between them, over which neither the one nor the other would ever set her foot. To make this plan workable, it was necessary that the two ends of the room should be each self-contained as regarded the necessary articles of household plenishing; and this, by the aid of Mr Ross and Peggy Fergusson, was duly accomplished. One of these articles was a big ha' Bible for Martha, to stand against that retained by Mary—in explanation of which I may inform the English reader that the old Calvinists had nearly as much faith in the size of their Bibles as in their contents. Nor was the strength of their faith altogether irrespective of the kind of cover, and the manner in which it was clasped. There was a great virtue in good strong calfskin—sometimes with the rough hair upon it; and if the clasps were of silver or gold, the volume had a peculiar merit. It was necessary, therefore, that Martha's Bible should be as big as Mary's; and the latter having been adorned by old Peter Jopp with silver clasps, so the former was equally orthodox in this respect.

And so the chalk line was drawn. The only difficulty regarded the fire; but this was got over by some ingenuity on the part of Peggy and a workman, whereby the grate was altered so as to hold two cranes; and so minute were the engineers, that the end of the chalk line came up to the hearth, dividing it exactly into two halves; so that each crane could be got at without overstepping the mark. This arrangement lasted through eleven years; and if to that period we add the five years of prior strife, this domestic war endured for sixteen years; nor, according to the report of Mr Ross and Peggy, with that of the good many curious visitors who contrived through various excuses to get a view of the domestic arrangement, was that magic line which thus separated two hearts once so loving ever transgressed; nay, it seemed to become a point of honour in the two maidens. They might read their Bibles on either side of it, and send their mute anathemas across it, so as to reach the unhappy non-elect; but not a foot of either ever trod upon the mark. The foot of time might dull it, but the ready hand of either revived the line of demarcation, even as the feelings were kept alive in undying vividness; all which may easily enough be conceived; it contravenes no law of nature; but I fairly admit that I must draw a strong bill on the credulity of poor modern haters of the Armenian kind, when I state what was on all hands acknowledged, that after the chalk truce —that is, for eleven years—the residents of this room, divided so against itself, never interchanged a word with each other. I freely admit that all traditions become incrusted by the marvellous. We do not reject port wine because it has undergone a certain process. Yes; but we do not swallow the crust, which is only deposited sugar. So be it; and you are welcome to your advantage, provided you admit that the raciness you admire is the consequence of the deposit; and so, in my case, you may reject the eleven years' silence of Martha and Mary Jopp, yet you cannot get quit of the tang of the reported marvel. For my own part, I am a little sceptical myself; but then I cannot prove the negative of a popular statement; and I rather doubt if there are many religions in the world which are founded on anything better than this defiance.

Towards the end of the eleventh year a new incident arose to change perhaps the tenor of this strange drama. Martha Darling, a daughter of the sister Margaret who went to India, was sent home to Mr Ross to be educated in Scotland, where she was to remain till the homecoming of her parents, who had become rich on the spoils of Cheyte Sing, or the Begums of Oude, or some other unfortunate Indian victim. The girl was generous, and full of young life; and Mr Ross became hopeful that by introducing her to her aunts some instinctive feelings might be called up in the breasts of the sisters which would break up the old congelation. He told her the story of the chalk line, and got a scream of a laugh for an answer, with the threat that she would force her aunts to embrace, and weep, and be friends. Next day the visit was made, and, designedly, without any intimation that the niece had arrived in Scotland. On opening the door, Mr Ross found the two ladies in that position in which he had so often before found them, each sitting stiffly on her own side of the chalk line, and looking out of her window into the close—for, as I should have stated before, the room was supplied by two windows.

"Your niece from India—only arrived yesterday."

No more time for prologue, for the girl flew forward, and taking her elder aunt round the neck, hugged her very lovingly after the Anglo-Indian fashion, and thereafter, making a spring over the line of chalk, she ran to Aunt Mary, and performed the same operation upon her, but with no emolliating result; the old petrefactions, which had become harder by the passage of every wave of time, were not to be dissolved or softened by the sparkling rill from the green sunny mountains. They looked strangely only because they looked unnaturally; but that was no reason why Martha the younger should change her nature, and so she rattled away, every now and then casting her eye, with a laugh, at the line of chalk.

"If I had you only in India," she went on, "where the natives, when they drink bang, dance such strange dances, you would laugh so. Shall I show you?"

And without waiting for an answer, she began to make very pretty but somewhat irregular revolving movements on the floor, whereby in a short time, by the rapid motion of her small feet, she contrived to efface the line of chalk.

"Now you can hardly see it," she proceeded with shortened breath; "and now, the nasty thing being gone, you are to cross and shake hands, and kiss each other."

But the good-natured girl's efforts were useless. The sisters sat as stiff in their chairs as if they had been the figures in a pagoda irresponsive to the dance of the worshippers. Even the confident will-power of youth, which under-estimates all difficulties, was staggered by the resistance offered to its efforts, and the young Martha was obliged to leave without attaining an object over which she had been dreaming the preceding night. Next morning the chalk line was renewed, the still air of the room in Burnet's Close had recovered its quietude from the oscillation produced by the young girl's laugh, and the demon of obstinacy sat enshrined in its niche which it had occupied for so many years; nor had the after visits of the younger Martha had any better effect towards the object that lay nearest to her generous heart. And now a month had passed; a particular morning rose—not marked by an asterisk in the calendar, and yet remarkable for opening with the thickest gray dawn that had been observed for a time. And here you may already see I am getting among the mists, where old Dame Mystery, with her undefined lines, is ready to assume the forms forecast by brooding fancy. The gloom in the old room still hung thick, as the two maiden ladies moved slowly about, so like automatons, each preparing her cup of tea. So sternly had custom occupied the place of primary nature, that it would now have appeared more strange and out of joint for them to speak than to be silent. And so, as the minutes passed, the gray mist of the morning gave way to the struggling rays of the sun, and now there was something to be seen—nay, something that could not be unseen. Nor this the less by token that the eyes of both our Martha and Mary were fixed as if by a spell upon that part of the wall over the mantelpiece. There was hanging bodily, in the old frame, and radiant with the old light, the real picture of their mother, for the possession of which they had sighed for sixteen years. We may easily conceive that it could not fail of an effect, even as free from the connexion of any mystery as to how it came to be there. But the question, if put by either to herself or her neighbour, could not be answered in any way consistently with natural causes, for neither of them had been out of the room—nay, neither had been in a condition which could have been taken advantage of by any one who wished by a trick to take them by surprise  Then how catching the superstitious when it plays into the hand of our fears! As they looked with spell-bound eyes on that apparition, and read once more the expression in that blessed countenance that spoke peace and love,—reproof enough to those who for so many long years had disobeyed her injunctions to treat each other as sisters, and love each other even as she loved them and they her,—they never doubted but that some unseen hand placed that picture there for the end of chastening their rebellious hearts, and bringing them back to that love which was enjoined even by Him whom they worshipped as the very God of Love. It seemed as if they shook as they gazed, and each one at intervals sought with a furtive glance the face of the other.

x

A charm was working among the old half-dead nerves that for years had quivered with the passions of the devil. The revived feelings of that olden time, when that mild loving mother was the centre of their affections and bond of love between themselves, were in a tumult below the hard crust of mutual hatred, that was breaking under the touch of the finger of God; they were both of the elect, since God took the trouble to chide them and recall them to their duty and their obedience. The relentings in the hard faces, the rising tears in the eyes of both, the tremors in the hands, all spoke eloquently to each other; nor did they speak in vain; they rose as if by sympathy. "O Martha!" "O Mary!" No more; the words were enough, and the two sisters were locked in the arms of each other, drawing long sighs, and sobbing convulsively.

A scene all this which, being apt to precipitate one of my disposition into the gushing vein, I must leave. I shall be on somewhat safer ground as I proceed to say what truth and probability equally require, that the paroxysm being over, and the two having begun, even as they had done of old, to make and sugar each other's tea, to butter each other's bread, and even to break each other's egg, or bone each other's small haddock—most delightful tricks of love, which selfishness knows nothing of, and cannot compensate by any means within its power,—they gradually began to doubt whether some kindly hand of flesh was not concerned in producing the phenomenon of the picture. They had both been sound asleep till nine o'clock, and Peggy Fergusson had in the gray dawn been in the room doing her duty to the fire. But what although the Indian elf, who had likely brought the picture home with her from India, had been put up by Mr Ross to a little deception, and had slipt in in the wake of Peggy, and hung it on the nail which had been so generously left by the old tenant? nay, these spinsters, apart from the delusion produced by the demon of obstinacy, were sensible women; and in the pleasant talk that now flowed like limpid water down a very pretty valley with flowers on either side they came to the conclusion, with—Oh, wonder!—a laugh fighting for utterance among the dry muscles, that the fact was just so as we have stated it. What then. Was not the effect admirable—yea, delectable?

A conclusion this which derived no little confirmation from the fact that the young Anglo-Indian came bouncing into the room about eleven o'clock, crying, in her spirited way, "Ah, I see it is all right," and yet never saying a word of the said picture; but, indeed, the fairy had some work to do other than of revealing the secrets of Titania to her victims, for she straightway set to work with a wet cloth to eradicate every trace of that devil-invented line of chalk which had so long kept asunder good amiable spirits. Nor was she contented with even this, for to satisfy her impish whims, she got her now changed aunts, nothing loth, to cross and recross the place of the now defaced line, till all notion of the division was taken out of their minds.

It is a pleasant thing for me to have authority to say that this miraculous change was not destined to be merely temporary. The flow from the once secluded fountains of feeling continued its stream—nay, it seemed as if the two old maidens could not love each other enough, and they had been often heard to confess that one hour of pure nature was worth all the sixteen years of factitious opposition to her dictates. So true it is that, let us deplore as we may the many ills of life, we shall never diminish them by damming up the fountains of feeling and driving the emotions back upon the heart. Then fortune favours those who are true to nature, who is the mother of fortune, and all other occult agencies. The nabob and his wife came home the next year, and set up a great establishment in our old city. The spinsters were gradually drawn out again into that world which they had so foolishly left—we use the word deliberately, for hermits carry with them into their cells a worse world than they leave behind, however unsteady, however cruel, and however vain, that may at times seem to be;—nay, we can say with a good conscience that our two sisters became the very darlings of a flock of young nephews and nieces; sometimes danced in a reel of ancient maidens; gadded gaily about; sipt their scandal, and helped like good citizens to spread the sweet poison; and passed many years as happily as can be the fortune of those who are contented to live according to the laws of nature.

*Ballantyne & Company, Printers, Edinburgh.*

www.ingramcontent.com/pod-product-compliance
Lightning Source LLC
Chambersburg PA
CBHW021208230426
43667CB00006B/606